REAL ESTATE SIDE HUSTLE

REAL ESTATE SIDE HUSTLE

Four passive
investing strategies to
BUILD WEALTH
beyond your day job

DEVON KENNARD

BiggerPockets®
PUBLISHING
Denver, Colorado

Early Praise for
Real Estate Side Hustle

"*Real Estate Side Hustle* is a game-changer for anyone looking to diversify their income and achieve financial independence…Kennard lays out clear, practical strategies for passive investing that are accessible to everyone, regardless of their current job. His unique perspective and proven track record make him the perfect author to guide readers on their own path to financial freedom."

—Henry Washington, author of *Real Esate Deal Maker*, cohost of the BiggerPockets *On the Market* podcast

"*Real Estate Side Hustle* is a blueprint for those who want to create a secondary income, but also a powerful statement for using your time today to control your time tomorrow…Devon inspires many to avoid the pitfalls of going broke and begin driving towards financial freedom."

—Jedidia Collins, NFL, CFP®, and author

"This book provides a comprehensive roadmap for aspiring real estate investors, outlining the four essential stages of the investment lifecycle. From securing that pivotal first deal to navigating the complexities of syndications and funds, the author offers a clear, insightful guide to unlocking sustainable wealth through real estate…A must-read for those seeking to maximize their returns and impact within the dynamic real estate landscape."

—David Shaw, real estate investor
with 25 years of experience

Real Estate Side Hustle: Four Passive Investing Strategies to Build Wealth Beyond Your Day Job
Devon Kennard

Published by BiggerPockets Publishing LLC, Denver, CO
Copyright © 2024 by Devon Kennard
All rights reserved.

Publisher's Cataloging-in-Publication Data
Names: Kennard, Devon, author.
Title: Real estate side hustle : four passive investing strategies to build wealth beyond your day job / Devon Kennard.
Description: Includes bibliographical references. | Denver, CO: BiggerPockets Publishing LLC, 2024.
Identifiers: LCCN: 2024938816 | ISBN: 9781960178688 (hardcover) | 9781960178695 (ebook)
Subjects: LCSH: Real estate investment--United States. | Real estate business--United States. | Personal Finance. | Investing. | BISAC BUSINESS & ECONOMICS / Real Estate / General | BUSINESS & ECONOMICS / Investments & Securities / Real Estate | BUSINESS & ECONOMICS / Personal Finance / Investing | BUSINESS & ECONOMICS / Real Estate / Buying & Selling Homes
Classification: LCC HD1382.5 .K46 2024 | DDC 332.63/24--dc23

Printed on recycled paper in Canada
MBP 10 9 8 7 6 5 4 3 2 1

DEDICATION

Dedicated to my incredible wife, Camille, whose unwavering love and support fuels my dreams.

To my cherished daughters, Camryn and Carsyn, whose smiles fill our home with joy and purpose.

Last but not least, my mom, dad, and older brother and sister for providing the foundation of stability I needed to confidently chase my dreams.

This book is a tribute to the love, strength, and resilience of my family, whose consistent belief in me continues to inspire every step forward.

TABLE OF CONTENTS

SECTION I
THE SIDE HUSTLE

SECTION II
INCREASE YOUR SPREAD

SECTION III
PREP FOR ACTION

SECTION IV
TAKE ACTION

SECTION V
SCALING UP

FOREWORD

When I married my husband Rich, we decided to make investing a priority. We met with a financial planner and did exactly what they told us to do. We set up our buckets of money, allowing various percentages to go to certain things (emergency savings, investment funds, charity, and those "dream" vacations). We thought we were pretty savvy.

Then in 2002, my husband was diagnosed with melanoma, a deadly skin cancer. The doctor was concerned that it had spread to his liver, and if that was true, Rich would have only six months to live. While thankfully the doctor was wrong and Rich is alive and well today, we learned that the money we set aside for emergencies could be depleted very quickly. In this case, it was gone in just six months.

I knew there must be a better way to ensure our financial future. Fortunately, I had a radio show, The Real Wealth Show, in San Francisco that I decided to use as a platform to learn the secrets of the wealthy. They must know something the vast majority of us don't know—otherwise all of us would be part of the 1 percent (which would likely be more than 1 percent with all of our success!). I was amazed at how willing these self-made millionaires were to share.

These people taught me the power of holding real estate for the long term. They explained that there are two ways to make money, through earned income and through investments.

They explained that a portion of your earned income should go to acquiring rental property as an investment. They talked about the tax benefits of owning real estate, the cash flow, but what I found most interesting was the long-term benefit of owning real estate. The ability to own property for the long term and reap the benefits of financial freedom was powerful! I wanted to use this information for myself—but I also wanted to share it with as many people as possible.

Rich and I made it our mission to teach as many people as we could on how to create financial freedom through real estate. We formed the RealWealth Network in 2003, to help share all these secrets of the wealthy with as many people as we could. Today, we have helped investors acquire over 7,000 rental properties and over $1.3 billion in real estate assets.

After being in business for over 20 years, I had the opportunity to interview Devon Kennard on The Real Wealth Show. I wanted to know how a professional athlete was able to become a successful real estate investor also. I was so impressed with his mission, which is to help more athletes invest their money before it's all gone. After all, professional athletes can't play forever. In fact, their careers can be cut very short in an instant if they have an injury. All too often, their hard-earned income disappears overnight, and they have nothing to show for it.

But it goes beyond just professional athletes or those with high-profile jobs. You and your money are important too. Devon shares how you can invest your money in real estate to ensure your financial future.

It's no secret that investing in real estate is popular these days. Any fix-and-flip reality tv show makes the job of buying old homes, renovating them, and selling them for a high profit look easy and fun. There's no shortage of Instagram stars standing by their hot cars, telling you that you can do it too. And now that new trends in real estate like sub-to and wholesaling are rising in popularity, many people are selling education products that claim it's easy too.

But the televised version of real estate investing is rarely the reality. Just like any business, it may look easy because the people who are doing it successfully have already made their mistakes and learned their lessons. There isn't a quick and easy way to invest in real estate. It takes skill, time, effort, and heart to find success as a real estate investor. And anyone who tells you differently does not have your best interest in mind.

Devon Kennard is not one of those people who will sell you a get-rich-quick scheme. He knows that building success as an investor takes time and hard work. And just like those who have found success, he has had to learn the hard lessons of real estate investing. In this book, he shares these lessons with you so that you don't have to struggle in your real estate investing endeavor.

So, where do you start? It seems like investing in real estate requires a lot of time. What if you simply don't have the time to invest in real estate? It can be a full-time job. But what if you already have a full-time job that you like?

There are millions of people who have careers they love and have worked hard to master. You may have spent years learning your trade and make a good living. You may not want a new job or want to quit your old job. But maybe you're thinking about retirement, and you want to make sure you are setting yourself up to live comfortably, to match the income you made while working full time. How can you invest in real estate, ensure your financial future, and keep your full-time job? Devon has those answers for you!

If you have met Devon, you know that he is a very large human. He's six-three and over 260 pounds of pure muscle. If you have had the chance to talk with him, you know that his heart is just as big. He is not only a savvy real estate investor but also authentic, caring, and seems to love every person he meets. As you read through this book you will notice that his intention is all about helping others (including you!) to grow and protect wealth in order to live life on your terms.

—Kathy Fettke,
coauthor of *Scaling Smart: How to Design a Self-Managing Business*, cohost of the BiggerPockets *On the Market* podcast, and CEO and cofounder of the RealWealth Network

PREFACE

$\mathcal{B}$efore we get into the thick of this book, I thought I would let you in on why I feel this book needed to be written and why I think I am the right person to write it.

The American Dream that we have been taught for many decades is now failing us. The idea that you can go to college, get a good job, buy a house, buy a car, and be stable and happy until your mid sixties when you can then retire and live happily ever after is not aligned with today's reality. Many Americans are getting to retirement age and realizing that their 401(k)s will not sustain them for the rest of their lives and they will need to continue to work; otherwise, they will outlive their savings.

Unfortunately, instead of making the changes they need to make in order to achieve their version of the American Dream, many people are staying the course, putting their heads in the sand, and just hoping it all works out in the end.

The old, outdated version of the American Dream needs to change. I think the real goal needs to be putting yourself in a strong financial position as soon as humanly possible—not waiting to grow your savings over many years until you hit retirement, and then start to live. Instead, life should be about going to work because you *want* to, not because you *have* to. To achieve this, you can't just depend on your job, career, or business. You have to leverage your current career to save and invest as much as possible.

Playing in the NFL gave me a unique perspective on this issue because I had a career that paid really well but could end at any moment. This reality motivated me to build a side hustle that could provide for my family and me, in case something happened. When that day did finally come where I could no longer play, I had complete control of my financial life.

Some of you likely have a job or career that is a bit more stable than an NFL player; but your mindset should still be similar. Your career may be great, but how can you get into a side hustle that will provide for you and your family even if you are let go, want to retire early, have health problems, or other unforeseen circumstance arises?

Well, guess what? Creating that side hustle even when you have a busy schedule is what this book is all about. I spent the last ten years figuring out how to invest in real estate (which I think is the best investment vehicle) as a side hustle to my day job. I want to share with you everything I have learned along the way so you can kickstart your own journey. Then, in the future, you can wake up with the peace of knowing that you have the choice to go to work or to stay home—either way, your lifestyle won't change because you're financially protected.

So much of the content about real estate today (whether it's books, social media, podcasts, or YouTube) is geared toward active investors who are spending significant time on their real estate portfolios. Over the last decade, I have consumed an embarrassing amount of this content. I've read just about every BiggerPockets book, I listen to multiple real estate podcasts regularly, I follow my favorite investors on YouTube, among other knowledge outlets.

My issue has always been, while the content and knowledge I have learned is great, it's been up to me to take that information and figure out how to translate it into an investing strategy that fits my lifestyle.

The truth is not everyone wants to or can leave their job and not everyone wants real estate to play a major role in their daily lives. For those of us who fit in that category, does that mean we can't or shouldn't invest in real estate? Of course not!

I refused to accept the idea that I can't build a real estate portfolio while thriving at my day job, which just happened to be playing in the NFL. So, I went on a ten-year journey learning as much as I could about different real estate strategies, and I figured out a way to invest in the same assets active investors were, but as my side hustle, not my main gig.

This book will free you from the idea that real estate has to demand all your time and give you the blueprint on how to see every real estate strategy from a passive perspective.

I am a firm believer that it is great to learn from your own mistakes, but if you really want to excel in life, you should learn from the mistakes of others. Well, I did much of the hard work on figuring out how to keep my career the main focus and build a real estate portfolio on the side. So instead of starting from scratch and trying to figure it all out on your own like I did, use this book to expedite that process and put you on the road to true financial freedom much faster!

SECTION I
THE SIDE HUSTLE

A side hustle allows you to take control of your financial destiny and build a future on your own terms.

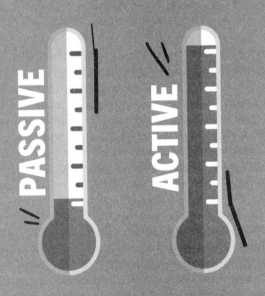

CHAPTER 1

LIFE ON YOUR TERMS

"Begin with the end in mind."

—Steven Covey, author

Over the last few years, I have stood idly by while listening to people denounce the idea that you can passively invest in real estate. Their argument? To succeed in real estate investing, you must be *fully* entrenched in the business. They do not believe you can actively find, fund, and manage properties—and ultimately build an empire—with only a few hours a week. I remember a direct message I received that blatantly told me I was a fraud for promoting that this kind of passive investing is real.

I understand their arguments. Honestly, I do. After all, no matter how you do it, real estate investing is not easy, and I agree with the active investors who say it takes time, energy, skill, and thoughtfulness. However, not everyone *can* or *wants* to become an active investor.

What's the difference? An active real estate investor devotes the majority of their working day to the business of real estate—they are fully entrenched. A passive real estate investor only allocates a small percentage of their day to real estate investing. This person spends most of their day on a career, job, business, or lifestyle unrelated to real estate.

If you are a physician who works forty hours a week, a stay-at-home mom who homeschools her children, a world traveler, or an entrepreneur who loves working on the business you built, you may not want to leave your job or change careers. However, you are still intrigued by the idea that investing in real estate can create a passive income stream and help you achieve your financial goals, create a lifestyle you crave, or both.

Even if you work or have something else going on, you *can* successfully and passively invest in real estate. I know this personally.

My interest in real estate started when I was a student at the University of Southern California and met Kyle Kazan, a USC alumnus who became a police officer in Los Angeles County, California. He and his wife, a teacher, earned modest salaries but started investing in real estate while still working their full-time day jobs. They purchased one small property and, over time, bought more. Today, they own more than 1,500 units and manage over 7,500 with a total of $2.75 billion in assets.

You may not want to become a real estate mogul like Kyle, and that's okay. However, his story intrigued me and showed me that becoming successful in real estate is doable, no matter your salary or how many hours you work each week. Right then, I wanted to learn everything I could about real estate and I needed to carve out the time in my busy schedule to do it.

I wanted real estate to replace—and even exceed—my NFL income one day so I could continue to pay my mortgage and other expenses and live my life on my terms later.

You can't start prepping for retirement when you're sixty-four. It takes years of planning, saving money, investing, and starting as early as possible with whatever time you have to give.

When I was playing football, my hectic schedule allowed me only five hours a week (I did most of that work on my day off) to dedicate to building my real estate empire. When I wasn't on the field, in the training room, studying football film, doing charity work, or being a husband (and later a father), I immersed myself in real estate and investing. My schedule was already stretched thin, but I refused to believe the naysayers who said I couldn't do it. Instead, I carved out an alternative route to my success throughout my nine-year career by using these few available hours a week to my advantage.

Here is an example of my daily schedule for the last decade.

6:30–7:15 a.m.	Lift begins
7:15–8:00 a.m.	Treatment for any injuries and independent film study
8:00–8:15 a.m.	Team meeting
8:15–11:00 a.m.	Offensive and defensive meetings
11:00–11:45 a.m.	Lunch and practice prep (dress, tape, stretch)
11:45–2:00 p.m.	Practice
2:00–3:00 p.m.	Post-practice meal, shake, treatment, cold/hot tub, and shower
3:00–5:00 p.m.	Post-practice film review with coaches
5:00–6:00 p.m.	Dinner and extra independent film or treatment
6:00 p.m.	Leave facility

This was my schedule from Tuesday through Friday. It didn't end there. Saturday was filled with meetings and walkthroughs, and then we had a travel day to our opponent's city. Most Sundays were game days, so we would arrive at the stadium four hours before kickoff. The game lasted for four hours and if it was an away game, we went straight to the airport.

Our only days off were Mondays, but we were still mandated to go in for treatment and rehab. That is also the day that most guys went in for an extra workout to relieve the soreness from the game. After I left the facility on Monday, I usually put in my five hours a week on real estate. If I had spare time any other day, I devoted it to family and leisure (can't be in grind mode twenty-four seven).

I retired from the NFL in 2023 after playing with the New York Giants, Detroit Lions, Arizona Cardinals, and Baltimore Ravens.

I always found it interesting that most people looked at investing for retirement as putting money in retirement accounts and not touching those investments or getting any direct benefit from them for twenty, thirty, or forty years.

From my perspective, you can invest in real estate and reap the benefits of cash flow and tax advantages today while still owning appreciating assets that can provide for you forty years down the line as well. When people say you can't have your cake and eat it too, I always think *why not*? Why does it have to be save for retirement the traditional way and accept the fact it won't help you today when there are investments out there that can provide for now and later?

As of January 2024, my real estate investment portfolio includes twenty-one real estate units (a mix of single-family and smaller multi-family properties) in the U.S., over forty real estate syndication investments as a limited partner, and over $3 million lent through my private lending company, 42 Solutions. You definitely do not need a portfolio of this size or larger. Many people accomplish all their dreams with way less than this. Also, do not forget that it took me ten years to get my portfolio to this size. Now I spend about twenty hours a week on my investments, but this is because I fell in love and want to do it for the rest of my life now. Remember, though, that all of my success thus far started with only five hours a week. You can start with two, five, ten, or twenty hours a week, depending on what you have available, and grow from there, but the idea is to just start.

Even though you picked up this book, you might still be asking yourself, "I have a job, career, or business, so why do I need to invest in real estate?"

Here's why: As a professional athlete, I went to work knowing that my team and bosses were looking to replace me. It was in my face *every day*. The NFL—which in my circles stands for "Not For Long"—is always trying to replace a current player with another one who is younger, faster, stronger, better, and ultimately cheaper. It wasn't *if* they would do it but *when*. Knowing that I faced possible replacement just about every day changed my perspective on my career as soon as I signed my first NFL contract. The good news is that I considered this change in mentality an advantage for my future.

If you have a more traditional job, career, or business, you are probably operating under the assumption that *your* job is more secure than mine. You think that all you need to do is chug along, put money aside for retirement, not make any waves, and you will have that job for as long as you want.

But the reality is that everyone is in the same position I was in as an NFL player. It doesn't matter what your profession is, somebody or something is always trying to take your job. Maybe your boss is looking to replace you with someone younger, better, or cheaper. Perhaps a new technology is about to make your current position obsolete. If you own a company, a competitor may crush your business, or a lack of sales may force you to close up shop. Then there is the possibility that you or a family member suffers a sudden illness that derails your finances and your time. Maybe you want to take a sabbatical from work before you retire. Even if none of this happens and you love your job and get to do it for decades, eventually you will retire. Traditional retirement is also an end, and it still leaves the questions of whether or not you have saved enough money to cover the rest of your life and what happens if you didn't.

Statistics show that the average NFL career only lasts around 3.3 years. Looking back, I signed that contract when I was twenty-three years old, and if those statistics were going to be accurate, I would be lucky to play until I was twenty-six. Signing didn't guarantee me anything but a shot at playing that year and maybe two more ... and then what?

At a rookie symposium in 2014, when I first entered the league, former NFL running back Eddie George spoke to us. He shared the phrase that would become my career mantra, "Begin with the end in mind."

This phrase changed my mentality about my future and should change yours too. Understanding that your career will end sooner rather than later should force you to prepare for that day in a way that protects you and your family financially. Whether you love or hate your job, it's time to invest in your future and put yourself in a position to work because you *want* to, not because you *have* to.

So again, it doesn't matter what you do for a living or even if you only have five hours (or less) a week to make a change. Passive real estate investing allows you to take complete control of your life and your future. Once you put this blueprint I have created in place, it will be a relief to know that you are building toward having enough income to sustain your life no matter what happens. That's freeing. And that's what passively investing in real estate is all about.

Let's start by diving deeper into the difference between *active* and *passive* real estate investors.

Active Investor

Examples of active investors who devote their days to the real estate business include my friend James Dainard, who flips hundreds of Seattle properties every year. He also co-hosts the BiggerPockets podcast *On the Market*. There's also Henry Washington (whom I had the pleasure of meeting at BPCON 2023), who has been crushing it in real estate since 2015. He announced on social media that he plans to buy and hold over one hundred properties in 2024 in his local Arkansas market.

These guys all do fantastic work and have built tremendous empires, but none have another job outside of real estate. Every day, their sole responsibility is to grow and expand their portfolio. In simple terms, they *actively* live and breathe real estate.

Most active investors are working toward stepping back from their business. They want a company that only requires them to be an active participant for a while. They will grow the business until it can sustain itself.

With that in mind, I find it funny that so many active investors say it's impossible to invest passively when most are working toward the goal to one day be passive themselves.

It is important to point out that you *can* make more money as an active investor than a passive investor on a deal-by-deal basis. But it's not guaranteed. For example, let's say two investors compete for the same off-market property. The active investor found a property and put in an off-market offer of $100,000. A wholesaler (someone who finds off-market deals and brings them to investors for a fee) found the deal and brought it to a passive investor but charged them $110,000, with $10,000 being their fee. The active investor has the time and capacity to find deals like these and, simply by cutting the wholesaler out of the equation by finding the deal themself, saves $10,000 on this transaction.

Let's take this example a step further. The active investor bought this property for $100,000 and decided to renovate it with a budget of $50,000. The active investor has the time to go to building supply stores and buy the materials instead of having contractors do it and mark up the prices. So, all in, their rehab costs are now $40,000, not $50,000. In comparison, a passive investor is much more reliant on their contractor. Fortunately, they found a good one that gets good pricing on the materials and labor. However, the passive investor was not able to bring the cost below the $50,000 budget because they still needed to pay the contractor for the time it took to pick up the materials and deliver them to the property. In simple terms, a passive investor will pay a premium for simply not handling it themself, and the renovation total stays at $50,000. The active investor saves $10,000 by playing a bigger role in the investment.

I can go on and on here. There are many ways that active investors leverage their strongest asset—time—to increase their investment return in a way that passive investors cannot.

You might suddenly agree with active investors who don't believe in passive investing, but keep reading because I'm about to show you a new way of thinking.

Passive Investor

As mentioned before, passive investors allocate a much smaller percentage of their day to real estate investing compared to active investors.[1]

Examples of passive investors include Chad Carson (author of *The Small and Mighty Real Estate Investor*), who owns and manages a sizable real estate portfolio but takes his family abroad for extended periods of time; Dave Meyer (author of *Start with Strategy* and host of the *BiggerPockets Real Estate Podcast*) works for BiggerPockets and owns a real estate portfolio that allows him to control his day-to-day schedule and lifestyle; and then there's me, someone who built a portfolio of real estate investments while playing in the NFL.

The common thread among all three passive investors is that our day-to-day lives are independent of the real estate industry. We have other things going on that take precedence but built our real estate business specifically so we can control how much time it demands from us.

Now, let's talk money. Yes, an active investor can potentially make more money than a passive investor on a single deal, but passive investors cannot or do not want to work like an active investor. We think differently about our money, investments and time.

Doing the work an active investor does to find a property at a significant discount or force equity with a major renovation was impossible for me when I was in the early days of my career and maybe for you too. You're busy with a forty-hour work week (or more) or with a lifestyle that doesn't provide that kind of time. On top of that, you are not yet equipped with the knowledge and resources to handle a complicated real estate deal.

I wanted to focus my time and energy on my NFL career—a dream come true for me—and make as much money as I could there. I knew I could leverage that money to buy real estate in ways that fit my lifestyle. My investments have always made a good return, but when I was starting, I did not buy properties that needed a lot of work. I simply did not have the time or the expertise to invest in a fixer-upper.

The moral of the story here is that passive investors are not competing with active investors. As I said, we are playing a completely different game. Passive investors have different goals and priorities compared to the active investor. What is a good deal to them may not be a good deal to us because maybe it takes too much time—something we don't have

---

1 Learn how to find, vet and invest in real estate syndications with PassivePockets, BiggerPockets' home for passive investing, www.PassivePockets.com.

to give *or* don't want to give. What may be a good deal to us may not be to them because they believe they can leverage their time to make a larger return.

Yes, an active investor might make more money than I could on the same property, but I kept my time and flexibility. Therefore, I was able to stay focused on football, which, at the time, provided a much larger return than the extra $10,000 I could have made on that example property above by being more active. Essentially, the extra hours it would have taken me to save $10,000 were not worth it in my eyes. Instead, I would make that money up in other ways, and by not devoting too much of my time to one deal, I was able to balance multiple deals at a time and scale even faster—as you will see throughout this book.

Stealing Time

So, how much time do you actually need to allocate to become a passive real estate investor? That is up to you and your lifestyle. You make the rules and live on your terms.

Can you manage to dedicate five hours a week with your schedule? Ten? Twenty? Be realistic with what you can give consistently. You do not want to overcommit and then not keep up with it. Commit to that number every week from here on out. Deal? Deal.

Maybe you are convinced that you do not have time to do anything else but read this book. That's a start too, but we all have the same twenty-four hours in a day. How you manage them determines how fast you become a successful passive real estate investor. Let me show you examples of where you can steal time you didn't think you had.

Are you a firefighter or a medical professional working a twenty-four-hour shift followed by a few days off? I'm sure you can find a few hours in those forty-eight to dedicate to learning. Are you a stay-at-home mom? While your child is napping, dedicate an hour a day to work on your debt or look up properties for sale in your neighborhood. Are you driving kids to school? Listen to the *BiggerPockets Real Estate Podcast*. Leave the housework one night while you do something to better your future. It will be there tomorrow, trust me. Are you a hardworking entrepreneur who dedicates sixty hours a week to building that business? Make it fifty-five hours and use those extra five for passive real estate investments.

Here are a few other ways where you can find the time to work on becoming a passive real estate investing success:

- Forget about streaming the latest, hottest TV shows for now, and use that time for you.
- Are you waiting at the doctor's office? Bring this book and take notes or scroll property sites on your phone.
- Are you stuck in traffic or commuting to work? Listen to money management podcasts.
- Wake up an hour earlier.
- Go to bed an hour later.
- If you get one, use your lunch hour wisely.
- Say no to time-sucking invitations or activities that are not your priority.

Later, we will learn even more about what you can get done during these free hours. For example, before you purchase your first property or investment, you must become familiar with the language of real estate so you can talk the talk and walk the walk. You will also take steps to improve your financial literacy and get your finances in order.

Early on, I put myself on an aggressive schedule to learn about real estate. Instead of downloading the newest rap album, I listened to podcasts on my way to work. During my cardio sessions, I ran on the treadmill while listening to a financial audiobook (for me, it makes my workouts go faster). I scheduled phone calls in the car or during my lunchtime. You *can* steal time and be intentional about it.

As a rookie in the NFL, I found a few hours a week to study the language and the market, but I didn't have more time than that to manage properties, fix leaky faucets, and collect rent. Eventually, I would begin investing and building teams to do that work for me, but it all took time, and I had to start somewhere. You must start somewhere too.

I didn't have a blueprint for success. Initially, I was insecure and didn't receive validation from anyone that what I was doing was right. I feared losing money, and everyone kept pushing me toward other investments (specifically the stock market). But I learned and listened to my gut about what was right for me. It took time and many mistakes to get me where I am today. This is my blueprint for you so that you have more knowledge and confidence than I did when I initially started. My goal is for you to use this blueprint to put yourself on the fast track to dominating as a passive investor. It's time to begin with *your* end in mind.

CHAPTER 2

THE PASSIVE INVESTOR'S MINDSET AND RESOURCES

"This sh*t is chess; it ain't checkers."

—Denzel Washington, *Training Day*

When I first started learning about real estate, I kept running into the same problem—I didn't know what the best path was to take.

I read every real estate book I could get my hands on and, at first, wanted to do it how the authors told me to. For example, I would read about a guy who successfully flipped five homes a month, and I thought, "Maybe I should do that."

I listened to a podcast featuring a woman who became wealthy by buying multifamily apartment buildings and starting her own real estate syndication, and I thought, *Maybe I should do that.*

I networked and took meetings with investors and heard about how they invested, and I thought, *Maybe I should go that route.*

I learned a lot, gained great insights into the real estate industry, developed strategies I could implement, was introduced to software I could use, and so much more. But even with my newfound knowledge, there was a major disconnect for me. I realized that most of the content I was taking in on real estate investing was geared toward people who are seeking to become *active* investors.

I didn't have time to knock on doors or make one hundred cold calls a day or one hundred offers a month, be the general contractor on my own fix-and-flip, negotiate a deal with a seller, handle all the property management duties, etc. I didn't want to think about how much a kitchen remodel would cost on a mid-level rehab project, how I could save 8 to 10 percent on gross rent by being my own property manager, or how I could save a few dollars by buying the material myself instead of hiring a general contractor. I was too busy focusing on sacking Aaron Rodgers, Tom Brady, Dak Prescott, or Matthew Stafford every weekend.

I wanted to become a real estate investor, but this made me feel as if I were banging my head against the wall and forcing a square peg into a round hole. I was beginning to feel helpless.

After my rookie season finished, it finally hit me that active investors were playing checkers while I (a wannabe passive investor) needed to be playing chess. In other words, we were each playing a different game. With the knowledge I was gaining, I felt obligated to be the flipper guy, the BRRRR (buy, rehab, rent, refinance, repeat) guy, or the syndicator guy, but none of those traditional roles were for me because they were better suited for active investors. I didn't want to be them. I had to find another way.

We already know that the biggest difference between an active and passive investor is the time they are willing or able to put in. An active investor also measures every investment opportunity by two major metrics —what is the return on my time and money, and is it worth the risk? While time is an active investor's superpower, it's the passive investor's kryptonite. I can look at the same deal, but my most important metric is the amount of time it is going to take from me. Is it possible to do this deal in the amount of spare time that I have? If it is, great. If it isn't, then it doesn't matter how good the investment opportunity is because if it's not something I can reasonably manage myself passively, then it's not a deal for me.

Therefore, any active investor and I will never see an investment from the same vantage point. I needed to play this game differently. If time wasn't my superpower, what was it? Once I understood and accepted the fact that I didn't need to be in competition with or follow the lead of active investors, my eyes opened, and I saw the passive investor's mindset more clearly.

The passive investor's mindset about each deal can be boiled down to this: the perfect deal. The perfect deal has three components:

- It is passive.
- It cash flows.
- It appreciates well.

If you find a real estate opportunity that hits all three of these markers, that's what I call the Passive Trifecta. The major difference between what a passive investor wants in comparison to an active investor comes down to whether it is passive or not. For a passive investor looking to build a side hustle, the first and most important factor in analyzing a deal is whether or not it is passive, while an active investor is not concerned with that at all.

The Passive Trifecta is exactly what I wanted: investments or deals that only took five hours a week of my time or less (passive) so I could focus on football, cash flowed well (for me that's 8 percent or more—we will talk about that later) and, I believed, would appreciate well (appreciation refers to the increase in value of an asset over time).

Every investment opportunity that came across my desk got this one-minute evaluation of the Passive Trifecta. If it hit all three bullet points, it was 100 percent worth diving into further and trying to make happen. A good example of such a deal was my purchase in 2023, a six-unit property in St. Petersburg, Florida. I had a team in place that found me the deal, a contractor I trusted to renovate the entire property, and a property manager who came with a great track record, so I evaluated the property with the Passive Trifecta checklist:

- ☑ **Passive:** I had a team in place to handle every aspect of the deal for me. Check.
- ☑ **Cash Flows Well:** In real estate, investors use a standard 1 Percent rule as an investment strategy. This rule states that a rental property's monthly income should be at least 1 percent of the purchase price. The formula is to divide the projected monthly rental price by the purchase price of the property. I was all in on this deal at about $1.1 million. After reviewing the rental comps with my property manager, we estimated that the gross rent would be almost $11,000 per month (once stabilized).

$$\$11{,}000 \div \$1{,}100{,}000 = 0.01 \text{ or } 1\%$$

This hits the 1 Percent rule.

In many markets today, the 1 Percent rule is dead and very few if any properties meet this rule. But I have found it's still a good marker to judge a property's cash flow potential. For instance, if a property in a desirable market like Arizona misses the 1 Percent rule but hits 0.8 percent, I may still be interested. However, if it only hits 0.5 percent, it's probably a deal I will immediately stop considering.

In the example above, if the rent was $9,000 instead of $11,000, that would reach the 0.8 percent mark and may be worth looking into ($9,000 ÷ $1,100,000 = 0.008 or 0.8%).

☑ **Appreciates Well:** Lastly, because I could buy the property at such a discount (due to its distressed state) and force equity (add value to a property by renovating it), I was already walking into a ton of equity. The St. Petersburg location was also a prime real estate area that I could reasonably assume would appreciate well above average. Check.

This deal hit the Passive Trifecta for me, so I moved forward.

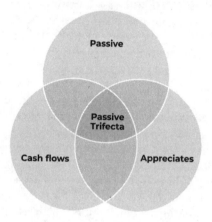

Of course, not every deal will hit the Passive Trifecta, so it's important to know your non-negotiables. At this point, I hope you agree that passive should be your number-one non-negotiable. With that in mind, if I come across a deal that hits two out of three checkmarks—let's say that it's passive and cash flows great but I don't think it will appreciate well—do I still consider it? Actually, yes, I still do because I value a good cash return.

Devon, did I hear you right? You will take on a deal that doesn't have much upside of appreciation? Yes. I have no problem holding a good cash-flowing property for ten or more years, even in a market that doesn't appreciate well. That's because the value of that asset will still go up over time, even if there isn't a better-than-average appreciation upside. I am comfortable playing the long game and letting an asset appreciate slowly, especially if the cash flow will be there year after year. The properties I own in Kansas City are a great example of this. I have averaged more than my goal of an 8 percent cash-on-cash return (CoC—the difference between the amount of money you invested in a property and what you earn annually on that property) year over year on these properties since I purchased them, but the appreciation of these properties has been low.

Also, a passive deal that I am confident will appreciate really well but the cash flow is below par can still be a great opportunity because it can help to grow your net worth exponentially. Below par does not mean that the property doesn't cash flow at all. I do not believe buying a property that has a zero or even negative cash flow is a good decision. The first property I purchased in Arizona is a great example of this. My CoC has been about 5 percent—below my goal of 8 percent or higher—but the property has almost doubled in value in five years. On deals like this, I will parlay that equity from appreciation into future investment opportunities (we will talk about how to do to this later). I do consider deals like that.

However, I draw the line on deals that have an incredible cash flow and the potential to significantly appreciate but require a lot of my time and effort. I have said no to many of these opportunities because time is my non-negotiable. For example, I could buy an Airbnb property in Scottsdale, Arizona, that will cash flow well because Scottsdale is a great market. As long as I find a property to buy at below-market value, there is no doubt that the property will appreciate. But I would need to manage the property and deal with bookings and constant guest turnover, and that is not something I am willing to do. I have—and will continue to—turn down investments like this that offer a great return but take too much of my time.

As a passive investor, you must determine your metrics and what you consider a good passive opportunity. Then look at every opportunity through that lens.

Now that I knew what my passive investor mindset needed to be, I was still left with the burning questions: How do I build my real estate portfolio passively? What will be *my* superpower if it's not time?

It took a few years to identify my strengths and how I could leverage them effectively to become a great passive investor. They are:

- Capital
- Knowledge
- Team
- Processes

Capital

You have a day job, career, or business that you want to continue—at least for now—while you invest in real estate passively. Hopefully, you have some money put aside from working so hard—your capital—to invest. If you don't, you will need to pay extra close attention to the next couple of chapters where we work on fixing this, something I call increasing the spread, the difference between the amount of money you earn and the amount of money you spend. Your capital is your first and most important superpower.

In addition to buying your own properties, you can use that capital for other investing opportunities. For example, you can become a private money lender to an active investor. You might know someone who is fixing and flipping homes. You can lend your money to that person and charge them anywhere from 10–20 percent interest. Remember, a passive investor thinks about how to leverage the capital you have into quality deals that allow you to remain passive.

For example, before my second season with the New York Giants, I wanted to invest in an affordable property. But if you know anything about the cost of living in New York City, you know that it is one of the higher-priced markets in the country. The median home price in New York City is $1.3 million and $649,000 for the entire state. The only states with higher median prices are Hawaii and California.[2]

I leveraged my network and met another investor who introduced me to a more affordable market in Indiana. Based on this information, a teammate and I bought a single-family house together in Beech Grove, Indiana. We each put $12,000 down on a three-bedroom, two-bath home that cost a modest $86,000. It was a turnkey property, which means it didn't need any work, and it came with a tenant already living in it. Immediately, we earned a profit of a few hundred dollars each month after our expenses were paid. It was a small amount, but it was something. I knew the more I invested, the more passive income I could make, which led me to where I am today.

If you are part of the BiggerPockets community already (if not, join me and 3+ million other investors at www.BiggerPockets.com to access free resources, build your network, and take action), you likely already know that it is possible to buy properties with no money down. There have been many books written on how to do it, but the major thing to

---

2   David McMillin, "Median Home Prices in Every State," *Bankrate*, January 3, 2024, https://www.bankrate.com/real-estate/median-home-price/#expensive-states

note here is that capital is a passive investor's superpower, but interestingly, it does not have to be only your capital. There are two main capital sources you should use as an investor: your capital and debt (which can include OPM—other people's money).

Your capital is pretty straightforward. You make good money at your job and save as much of that money as possible to invest in properties. The biggest problem with using your own capital is that many investors don't have enough cash to invest in real estate. Many industry experts would also argue that even if you did have enough money, you should still use leverage. If you do have enough capital, it will eventually run out if you use all of it to buy properties, and then you can't buy any more. I don't recommend you use only OPM, especially when starting out. It's valuable to have some skin in the game. Investing your own capital buffers you from being over-leveraged and exposed to higher risk.

There are many ways to use debt to get into real estate, but we will review some of the most common:

1. **Traditional Mortgage:** Typically given through a bank or credit union, a traditional mortgage is usually a thirty-year fixed-rate loan that is in your name. As a passive investor with a W-2 job, you will (hopefully) qualify for these loans and can buy up to ten properties using this traditional method of financing.

2. **Hard Money/Private Money Loans:** Hard money loans typically come from large institutions/companies. Private money loans come from individuals or smaller limited liability corporations (LLCs). An LLC is a business structure that offers limited liability protection and pass-through taxation and exists as a separate entity from its owners. It's important to note that, when you are a borrower, hard and private money lenders expect to do these loans to LLCs, not individuals. If you don't already have an LLC, you will need to start one to apply.[3]

   The pros of using hard and private money loans are the quick access to funds and the flexibility of the loan terms.

   The cons are that the loan terms are very short (six to eighteen months typically), and interest rates are very high (typically double digits). This is why these loans are used most commonly by fix-and-flip investors and people looking to BRRRR, who both have shorter investment strategies and large enough spread that

---

[3] You can find a checklist on how to start an LLC on the BiggerPockets website at www. BiggerPockets.com/bookllc

they do not mind the higher interest rates. They also value the fact that they can close much faster on these loans than most other debt options.

3. **Debt Service Coverage Ratio Loan (DSCR)**: Some investors do not qualify for traditional loans and/or have exceeded the ten-loan maximum. If that's the case, DSCR loans are a great alternative. These are loans based solely on the projected cash flow from a property in comparison to the purchase price. DSCR lenders want to make sure that the net operating income (NOI) of the property can cover the monthly debt payment and more. They will typically lend up to the amount that the NOI will cover. Because these loans are based on the income covering the loan amount, they do not take into account your personal finances—that is a feature many investors love. Similar to hard and private money lenders, DSCR lenders also prefer to do loans to LLCs, not individuals, but there are, of course, exceptions to this. The DSCR interest rates are competitive with traditional loans and even have similar thirty-year loan terms.

4. **Portfolio Loans**: For more advanced investors who own many properties, portfolio loans allow you to take out one loan for multiple properties. I owned six properties in Cleveland, Ohio, that I originally bought with cash. After a few years of owning them, I decided to take out a portfolio loan in which all six properties would be refinanced under one loan on a thirty-year fixed mortgage. Having one loan for all six properties instead of six separate loans was the perfect solution for me and was much more manageable.

Portfolio loans are done through an LLC, not your personal name. They can also be thirty-year mortgages, and the interest rates are typically just a bit higher than traditional loans.

However, one major con of portfolio loans is that when you decide to sell, it's a headache. You either need to work with a lender to break the loan apart so you can sell each property individually, or you will need to find a buyer who will buy all the properties together. I learned this the hard way when I wanted to sell those Ohio properties. I eventually sold them as a package deal at a discount to save the difficulty of selling only one property at a time when they were all under the same loan. I probably could have sold them individually for more money, so I will certainly consider my exit strategies before I do my next portfolio loan. Lesson learned.

5. **Partners**: This capital source is straightforward—you partner with someone with money to invest. Many investors take on a partner to solve their capital needs. The biggest challenge is getting on the same page regarding strategy and risk tolerance. With a partner, you are splitting the risk, which can be a good thing, but you are also splitting the profits, so weigh the options on whether partnering really makes sense for you.

   Also, most people who partner with someone still need to use one of the other debt or OPM sources to purchase a property. For example, I partnered with my friend on our first purchase in Indiana, and we both put $12,000 down, but we still needed to find a loan to cover the remainder of the mortgage. I was the one who was approved for a traditional loan and put it in my name.

6. **Raise Capital:** You can also raise capital from other investors, use it to purchase a property, then provide the investors with a return on their money. You see this a lot in commercial real estate and syndicated deals. One of the best features of raising capital is that you can leverage OPM to buy much higher-priced properties and/or increase the number of deals you can buy.

   Let's say you have $100,00 to invest. You can only buy so many properties with $100,000, even if you are using another debt source. But if you find nine more people with $100,000, you have $1 million. Now you can use debt of $1 million to buy much more real estate. The main issue with raising capital is you are now responsible for other people's money and are required to report to them about the investment. So far, I have stayed away from raising capital because I view it as something that will take too much of my time. Asking people for money, managing that money, and then reporting regularly to everyone who gave me money are not passive activities, so I avoid this option.

7. **Creative Financing:** Many strategies are classified as creative financing, but I am only discussing the two that have been most popular over the past few years—seller financing and sub-to financing. Both use the seller's equity in their property as your OPM. In seller financing, the seller owns the property outright and is acting as the bank for you. In sub-to financing, the seller has a preexisting mortgage, and it will stay in place after you purchase their property, but you will assume the payments on that loan (see Sidelines on page 33 for further explanation).

Do a personal assessment of how much capital you have and have access to and which of the OPM strategies are best suited for you.

Personal Capital Assessment

1. How much capital do I have to invest?
2. What kind of property do I want to buy? (We will review options later, but if you know what you have in mind, put it here.)
3. How much do these properties cost in my niche market?
4. In addition to my capital, what sources do I need to tap into to buy this kind of property?

Once you have the answer to these questions, it's time to pursue the capital source you need.

The capital source you use is dependent on your financial situation and what makes sense for the type of investment you are buying. Once you know where your capital is coming from, you have arguably the strongest superpower of them all right in your back pocket.

In my opinion, the most effective way to invest passively in real estate is to have access to capital and know how to leverage it. Capital is what gets many passive investors into the investing game and taken seriously by other professionals. Think about it: If you are trying to buy properties and are looking for people to help you find deals, renovate units, and so on, but you have no money, those people will lose all interest in working with you. On the flip side, if you have access to capital and are ready to invest, you will be taken much more seriously.

We cannot talk about capital and different loan options without discussing risk tolerance. When you start to bring debt into the equation, you are adding inherent risk to the success of the investment because if you cannot pay the debt, you risk losing the property to the lender. Your risk tolerance is how much risk you are comfortable in taking on. Your answer to that greatly impacts the type of loans you should pursue and how much your loan to value, or LTV should be. The premise here is that the higher your interest rate is, the shorter the loan term should be. The more debt you take on, the higher your monthly payment will be, which increases the risk of your not being able to make the payments. When making a decision on what kind of loan and terms you will accept, be sure to make a decision that is aligned with the amount of risk you are comfortable taking.

SIDELINES

Is Creative Financing Thinking Like a Passive Investor?

Creative financing was a hot real estate topic in 2023 in large part due to how high the interest rates were at the time (peaking at the 8 percent range). Creative financing means finding alternative methods for funding the purchase of a real estate asset.

Many strategies could fall into the creative financing bucket, such as seller financing, sub-to, lease options, and so on. The two that were talked about most often were seller financing and sub-to.

Seller financing is when a property owner owns their asset free and clear and is trying to sell it. As the buyer, you negotiate with that seller to buy the property, but the seller acts as the bank and finances a portion of the purchase. For example, you buy a $500,000 property and agree to put down $100,000 at closing but ask the seller to finance the remaining $400,000. In return, you agree to pay a monthly payment to the seller until the balloon payment comes due, at which time you pay the remainder of the $400,000 back. Huge caveat here: When that remaining balance comes due is completely negotiable between borrower and the seller. I have seen deals where the balloon payment is due in two years all the way up to thirty years, similar to a traditional loan.

The benefits for the buyer of a seller-financed deal are they do not have to work with a bank at all, avoiding all the requirements and mandates that come with it. Sellers get to do business directly with buyers and negotiate terms that are favorable to them. Many sellers like seller-financed deals because they get to act like the bank and also collect monthly interest payments from the buyer for the length of the agreed-upon loan.

In most cases, there aren't many drawbacks to a seller-financed deal for the buyer. A seller may have the fear that the buyer will stop making payments. The good news is that the documents are still legally binding, so if a buyer stops making payments, the seller can still foreclose on the property and take ownership again. However, it's a headache many sellers don't want to bother with—that's why it is the main drawback.

The other creative financing strategy investors are taking advantage of is what's called a sub-to deal, in which you buy a property but the loan isn't paid off. It stays in the seller's name, and you take over the payments. Buying that same $500,000 property as a sub-to deal would look like this: The seller has a $350,000 mortgage at 3.5 percent interest, so you agree to pay $150,000 at closing and take over their loan.

Investors have been loving sub-to deals when interest rates were up to 8 percent because many deals were not making sense financially. But if investors can go into a deal and take over the current owner's loan at a 3.5 percent interest rate, all of a sudden that same deal makes a ton of sense.

For the seller, a sub-to deal makes sense if they are in distress and in jeopardy of losing their home or need to get out of their loan quickly. It can also work for them if their property is in really bad condition and will be hard to sell in the traditional manner. The sub-to strategy has drawbacks for both buyers and sellers. The buyer's drawback is that banks do not like sub-to deals, and if they find out about it, they can call the loan due at any point. This runs the risk that you will have to pay off the loan immediately. The biggest risk for the seller is that the buyer stops paying your loan with the bank. In this case, the loan is in your name, and if the buyer doesn't make payments, this could seriously impact your credit score.

When the real estate market hit a rough patch in 2023 in large part due to those interest rates we discussed, many active investors looked at creative finance opportunities and pivoted all or most of their business into finding and procuring seller-finance and/or sub-to deals. However, finding and negotiating these deals is much more challenging than buying homes the traditional way. Active investors have the time and resources to execute these deals, so they can double down and do more cold-calling and door-knocking and learn how to negotiate and pitch these creative deals to potential sellers instead of buying their homes the traditional way. These efforts may have only produced a few sub-to deals for them, but the effort was likely worth it.

On the flip side, a passive investor recognizes that these opportunities are great, but many don't have the bandwidth to execute a creative finance strategy by themselves. In most cases, the amount of time, research, and paperwork needed to be successful in investing this way does not fit the passive investor's buy box. If you are a passive investor and have a strong interest in creative financing, you need to make this a niche you are an expert in and create a team and process that allows you to execute this strategy but does not impede on your time limitations. Don't be discouraged, though. I know many passive investors who have found ways to source and execute on creative deals—check out Chad Carson, Justin Donald, and Gabriel Hamel. These are three investors who identify as passive but have a portfolio full of creatively financed deals. It is possible, just not easy.

I tell all my deal finders (the agents, investors and wholesalers) that I am interested in creative financing, and if they can find a good seller-financed or sub-to opportunity, I will certainly take a look at it and become a potential buyer. But as of 2024, I am one foot in and one foot out on creative financing. I would love to take down a creatively financed deal, but I am not willing to make that a focused niche and do not want to shift my entire investing strategy to this. I feel the risk is too great and it will eat up way more of my time. I also fear it will shrink the number of deals I have a chance at buying because there are far too many sellers who are not interested in either strategy.

If you want to learn more about creative financing, I recommend Pace Morby's book *Wealth Without Cash: Supercharge Your Real Estate Investing with Subject-To, Seller Financing, and Other Creative Deals.*

Knowledge

Knowledge is not just power; it's a superpower. You do not need to be the one who manages the flip or runs the syndication. As I mentioned in the last chapter, early on in your journey, you must invest time to gain the knowledge you need to understand the ins and outs of investing. Learning how major renovations are managed, how wholesalers find deals, how landlords manage tenants, and how to underwrite deals, will serve you well as you evaluate people with whom you will be working. Otherwise, you run the risk of being taken advantage of. Also, as you are networking and building a team, having adequate knowledge and understanding of real estate acts as an asset for you and allows you to build trust.

All that time I spent learning about real estate investing and how active investors were doing it was not wasted. The books, podcasts, and meetings paid off because although I did not want to do the tasks of an active investor, I was very knowledgeable of what those tasks were, the questions I needed to ask, the things I needed to watch out for, and so on.

I think the biggest mistake many people who are trying to become passive investors make is they never take the time to actually gain the knowledge of real estate. By not understanding real estate investing, they are really just gambling and hoping they get it right. (I break down twenty key terminologies and other concepts you need to know in Chapter 6.)

Team

As a passive investor, you will be adding experts to your team who will do the work for you that is typically done by active investors.

We will dive into this more in later chapters, but depending on the type of investment and asset class you are investing in, you will want to work with people who will help you. For example, a property manager is a must-have if you buy and hold properties yourself. If you plan to get into syndicated deals, an experienced investor who buys syndications for themselves is a must-have. If you plan to lend your money as a private lender, a lawyer and title agency are must-haves.

Your ability to identify the people you need on your team is critical. If you go at it alone, you risk making significant errors and turning a passive investment into an active one. The teams you put into place will be vital to your success as a passive real estate investor.

Processes

I have not met a successful passive investor who has not developed processes to get things done efficiently and help with checks and balances. This ensures that their investments are going smoothly.

- How will you communicate with the deal finders? Have a process for that.
- How do you keep track of a renovation? Have a process for that.
- How do you make sure the property manager is running proper background checks on potential tenants? Have a process for that.
- How do you remember when, as a private lender, your borrower's loan payment is due? Have a process for that.

To jump-start this for you, throughout this book, I will give you the blueprint of many processes I have put in place for myself over the last decade. The more processes you set up for every aspect of your passive investing portfolio, the easier it will be to manage your investments and, most important, the less time it will take.

SECTION 1 CONCLUSION

By now, I hope you have put down the active investor checker pieces and picked up the passive investor chess board. It is imperative that you play this new game and, to be a highly successful passive investor, look at your capital, time, processes, and knowledge from an entirely new mindset.

Now that we have established exactly what passive investors are and how they differ from active investors—we will embark on a journey throughout the rest of this book diving into the exact steps you need to take to become a thriving passive real estate investor. If you are looking for an easy path or a walk in a park where you do absolutely nothing and make millions of dollars, let me warn you now, you won't find that in the remaining pages of this book. But if you come with an open mind and are ready to take intentional steps based on actionable advice, then I know firsthand what impact this information can have on your life.

Luckily for you, I have consolidated everything you need to know about passive investing into what I like to call The Passive Investor Pyramid. The Passive Investor Pyramid has four levels: increase your spread, prep for action, take action, and scale up.

Let's start with Level 1!

SECTION II
INCREASE YOUR SPREAD

*You must **EARN** the right to become an investor.*

Scale Up

Take Action

Prep for Action

INCREASE YOUR SPREAD

A foundation of a house supports the structure. It holds a home up and gives it stability, and we all know that you can't build a house on a weak foundation, or it is at risk of collapsing. The same can be said for building a successful career in passive real estate investing. The foundation that gives your journey a sturdy structure is what I call increasing your spread.

Increasing your spread is what you need to do to be in a financial position to invest passively. As you increase your spread, you are earning the right to become an investor.

What does increasing your spread even mean, and how do you increase it?

Let's start with a simple math equation:

How much you make in a year (post-taxes) minus how much you spend in a year, equals your spread.

Calculate how much you earn in one year (after taxes) from your full-time job plus any side hustles. For example, let's say last year's total income was $100,000 (rounded off for ease of the example). Now calculate how much you spent in one year on everything, from household expenses to miscellaneous. For this scenario, we will use a total of $80,000.

The spread is $20,000.

$100,000	**$20,000**	$80,000
How much you make	**THE SPREAD**	**How much you keep**

$100,000 – $80,000 = $20,000.

After everything was bought and paid, you had $20,000 left.

Now that we know the spread, your number one priority as a passive investor is to increase this number as much as possible. The larger the spread between what you make and what you keep, the better position you are in to invest and reach financial stability outside of your day job or career.

Imagine what you could do as an investor if your spread was $25,000, $40,000, or $50,000. Increasing your spread allows you to reach true financial freedom and provide capital to build a real estate empire.

There are two ways to increase your spread, and they are super simple:

- Decrease your spending
- Increase your earnings

Even better, a combination of doing both is like putting a rocket on your back while on the path to increasing your spread. Let's see how you can accomplish this faster.

CHAPTER 3
UNDERSTAND EXPENSES

"Money is only a tool. It will take you wherever you wish, but it will not replace you as the driver."

—Ayn Rand, author and philosopher

*G*etting behind the wheel and on the road to successful passive investing in real estate is exciting, but this is your journey, not mine. As Ayn Rand said in the quote above, you are the driver, and how fast or slow you decide to drive on your investing journey is your call. Your decision will also be the direction you take your money, once you learn all the available options.

But as with any journey you embark on, it's wise to be thoroughly prepared to prevent any bumps along the way. Where are you going? How do you get there? What information do you need to take with you? What can go wrong? How do you make it so you have a much smoother ride?

On this journey, step one means taking a good, hard look at your current financial status, whether good, bad, or ugly. From spur-of-the-moment purchases at the mall to rent and credit card payments and everything in between, many transactions are done by just swiping your card, so you probably do not review bank statements as often as you should. This is a real estate book, not a personal finance book, but to become a successful passive real estate investor, you need to get a clear picture of how much you're spending.

Becoming intimately familiar with your expenses is vital to this part of your success. Can you tell me how much money you dropped last week at your favorite burger joint, on the trendiest fits, or spontaneous purchases at Target when you just stopped by for "one thing"? How much cash did you pull out of your wallet for your kid's school lunches or hanging out with friends that you didn't jot down? And what about the splurges at the nail salon because you had a hard week and wanted to treat yourself to something special?

Your Current Target Monthly Income

It's time to identify the average amount you spend every month. Once you identify what you spend on a monthly basis, that is your Target Monthly Income, or TMI (in this case, it's not "too much information"). Your TMI is the minimum income you need to earn each month to sustain your life as it is right now and the minimum income you'll need to eventually replace through passive investing. If you've never calculated this number or haven't done it in a while, this number will probably shock you. Most likely, your estimate of it is far from your reality.

For example, if you're spending an average of $60,000 per year on everything from your mortgage to groceries and lattes, you need to make, at minimum, $5,000 each month after taxes just to cover those expenses, plus any changes because expenses grow over time due to inflation. However, if your yearly salary is only $45,000 and you're spending $60,000, you have some work ahead of you. You are bleeding an excessive amount of money each month and cannot sustain this pace.

The good news is that if your salary is $100,000 and your TMI is $60,000, you are in a much better position with a spread of $40,000. This gives you healthy breathing space, but there might still be room for improvement before you begin investing.

If you are investing with a spouse or significant other, you should have them participate. You need to know their credit scores and background and have them gather all the same information. Based on the information you find, partnering with that person might not be the best financial decision, but you won't know unless you go through this process.

Now it's time to plug in your exact numbers to the TMI formula. Start by gathering all your account information from the last twelve months.

You need:

- Credit card statements
- Checking account statements
- Transaction statements
- Any other statements where you use money to purchase items, such as PayPal, Venmo, or prepaid debit cards
- Cash receipts, if you have any

You could review your spending over any amount of time—three months or six months, for example. But I prefer to review a year's worth because spending is never a straight line. You will spend more in some months than you do in others. For example, in the summer, your gas costs skyrocket because you trek to the beach every weekend while on summer vacation, and they spike again in November and December because of holiday shopping. This year in review will be an eye-opening look at your spending habits.

What You Make in a Year − **What You Spend in a Year** = **Your Spread**

Now add up how much money you spent over the last year on everything—all of it. Do not leave one penny out. Include all your bills and every time you ran through the drive-thrus on your way home and all the lattes that you bought. Once you have the total, divide it by twelve. This is your current TMI, your target total monthly income amount.

> **NOTE:** This is not factoring in what you should put aside for emergencies. A good rule of thumb I like to use for my emergency fund is about 5 percent of my TMI. So, if I spend $10,000 a month, I think it's smart to put $500 per month or $6,000 annually aside for life emergencies.

As I've mentioned before, I have a very conservative personality when it comes to money, so I make sure to round my TMI total up and work off that number. For example, if it's $4,500, I'm rounding it up to $5,000. Why? Because I might miss some items, and I want to be as realistic as possible.

Look at your TMI. Do you feel a punch in your gut? Maybe in the back of your mind, you thought, "I'm only spending about $5,000 per month on everything. This number is not that bad." Maybe not, but if you make $50,000 a year working in New York, you are taxed approximately

$11,596 (if you are filing as a single person without write-offs). That means your net pay is roughly $38,404 yearly or $3,200 monthly. If your TMI is $5,000, you can do the math pretty quickly to discover that you're spending more than you're earning.

On top of this, if you see that you are charging purchases to credit cards because you do not have enough cash, it is time to face the fact that your spending needs to be reeled in before you move forward; otherwise, you are heading for severe financial trouble. In that case, real estate investing will have to wait until you control this.

And no, spending problems do not just affect those who earn under $100,000. High-wealth earners who make more than six figures are huge culprits in spending beyond their means. It doesn't matter if you make a million dollars a year if you also increase your expenses exponentially. Do not skip this step, no matter how much you make or where you are in your financial journey. Learning your TMI is a prerequisite to becoming an effective passive investor.

Understanding what your TMI is, why it is essential to have this number, and knowing what to do with it will propel you into the next step of your passive real estate investing journey. Now that you have your TMI number, let's look more closely at your expenses and then, if needed, what can be done to improve your financial situation.

My TMI number is: _____

Date: _____

Fixed Expenses

There are two types of expenses: fixed and variable. Think of fixed expenses as your needs. The six major fixed expense categories relevant to most people are housing, transportation, other debt, healthcare, food, and, last but not least, personal.

No matter who you are, where you live, or how old you are, you will always have non-negotiable expenses. Let's break them down:

- **Housing:** Whether you pay a mortgage or rent, everyone has a housing expense. You may also have other housing expenses, such as homeowner's or renter's insurance, property taxes, repairs and maintenance, HOA fees, lawn care, pool care, pet fees, utilities, internet, cable, and so on. Remember, some of these expenses are paid semiannually or annually, so find the yearly amounts and divide them by twelve.

- **Transportation:** As with housing, everyone spends money on some form of transportation, whether you own or lease a vehicle or pay for the train, bus, or car services. Include all the auxiliary expenses that come along with your vehicle, such as car insurance, title and registration, oil changes, tire rotation and replacement, repair and maintenance expenses, and so on. Again, some expenses may not recur every month—for instance, you may only get two oil changes a year—so total the amount you paid for oil changes in one year and divide by twelve.
- **Other debt:** This fixed expense is relatively straightforward. Total all your debt from credit cards, student loans, and any other personal loans that need to be paid back.
- **Healthcare:** Add up how much you are paying for health insurance for you and your family. Don't forget to include copays for doctor visits and medications.

> **TIP:** Use this time to ensure you have enough health insurance for you and your family. If your health insurance premium is high, consider shopping around for a less expensive medical plan that covers your immediate healthcare needs.

- **Food:** Everyone must eat, so total how much you spend on groceries. We're not talking about GrubHub, DoorDash, or fast food. This category is just for food you bring home regularly to feed your family. (The DoorDash and Grub Hub receipts will go into a different category.)
- **Personal:** Now add the expenses that are priorities, just for you and your family. Your personal fixed expenses will look different than mine. For example, I am in the public eye now, making speeches and doing interviews. My wife is a Realtor who meets with clients, so our personal trainer, haircuts for me, and the nail salon for my wife are our personal spending priorities. So are our kids' extracurricular activities.

I know a writer who reviews television shows and films and spends approximately $150 monthly on streaming services. It's part of her job and allows her to bring home an income, so this is a personal expense.

You might have an art hobby and spend $200 a month on supplies, and this is extremely important to you. You hope one day to make a living by selling your art, causing this to be a non-negotiable expense that goes in the fixed category.

Unless you have to give these items up because you can no longer afford them, there are certain fixed expenses that you value and are not willing to sacrifice. Put those here.

Now that you know what the six major fixed expenses are, use the chart below to list your totals:

HOUSING

Rent or mortgage: _____

Homeowner's or renter's insurance: _____

Utilities (electricity, water, gas): _____

Property/school taxes: _____

HOA fees: _____

Home warranty: _____

Security systems: _____

Pool maintenance: _____

Lawn care: _____

Other: _____

Total: _____

TRANSPORTATION

(Add a second section if you own more than one car.)

Car payments: _____

Car insurance: _____

License renewal: _____

Registration: _____

Oil changes (monthly average): _____

Tire rotation or replacement (monthly average):

_____

Other maintenance: _____

Gas (monthly average): _____

Other: _____

Total: _____

OTHER DEBT

Credit card debt: _____

Student loan debt/tuition: _____

Miscellaneous debt: _____

Total: _____

HEALTHCARE

Health insurance premiums: _____

Doctor visit copays: _____

Medication: _____

Supplements: _____

Other: _____

Total: _____

FOOD

Groceries: _____

Other: _____

Total: _____

PERSONAL

1: _____

2: _____

3: _____

4: _____

Total: _____

Total Monthly Fixed Expense Amounts:

$ _____

Variable Expenses

Think of variable expenses as your wants. They aren't always consistent in cost but are purchased more by choice than necessity. For the most part, variable expenses are those you're not married to and could be cut if necessary. Black Friday shopping only happens once a year, so it's variable. The videogame you bought for your son's birthday is a variable expense.

Other examples include your favorite pumpkin spice lattes, fancy bottles of wine, and the expensive steak dinner you tell yourself that you deserve because you worked so hard and didn't have time to cook. It also includes book club memberships, subscriptions to streaming and food delivery services, and tickets to those must-see concerts.

An easy way to determine your spending on variable expenses each month is to subtract the fixed expense total from the current TMI you already figured out. Whatever is leftover is what you are spending on variable expenses.

Every person's list will differ because of personal preferences, but here is a partial list to get you started. Include everyone you pay for, too. If you have children or are responsible for the care of someone else, include their costs for clothing and entertainment, etc.

Entertainment (concerts, movies, etc.): _____

Personal care (massages, facials, etc.): _____

Hobbies (supplies, collections, etc.): _____

Clothing: _____

Pet Sitter: _____

Jewelry, etc.: _____

Travel/vacationing: _____

Dining out: _____

Alcohol: _____

Gym or club memberships: _____

Cable or streaming packages: _____

Miscellaneous: _____

When you look at this list, which variable expenses do you value the most? Be honest. You might be spending way more than you realize on things you don't even value or use. For example, many people spend much more on luxury sportswear and athleisure products than they really should. Are the products worth it? Do you even use them? Reevaluate each expense and its worth before going forward.

Every expense, whether fixed or variable, is about choice. For example, when I was first drafted in the NFL, I wasn't one of those rookies who ran out and bought a brand-new car or a house or a bunch of gold jewelry. Seriously.

Instead, I had the car I drove in high school, a Kia Sorento, shipped to New York for me to use. I drove it my entire first season. I didn't need a new car or want one. I already had a car, so I decided to use it while I waited to see what being in the NFL was all about.

Word spread about the New York Giants rookie who shipped his high school car to use, so I capitalized on the attention. The following year, I worked out an arrangement with a local dealership to drive one of their Kias for three more years, and I posted photos of me doing it. So now I was getting paid to drive a brand-new car while most of my peers had purchased or financed expensive vehicles.

When I was living in New Jersey, where the New York Giants facility and stadium are, I could have purchased a home or rented a condo on the water in Hoboken like many of my teammates did. However, renting there would have cost me almost $2,000 more than a nice enough apartment in nearby Secaucus (literally a few miles away), so I rented there instead. I closely monitored my fixed and variable expenses from the day I signed my contract.

In the off-season, I would return home to Arizona. With my salary, I could have afforded to rent a home in the middle of Scottsdale near all the nice restaurants, bars, and clubs (I deserved it for achieving my goal, right?). Still, I made a financially smarter decision: to stay at my parents' house for a few months.

I was happy to make these sacrifices, but I got grilled by others who just didn't understand. *Bro, why don't you buy a nicer car? DK, why aren't you living in Hoboken? Why aren't you renting in Scottsdale?* Through the eyes of everyone else, I was an NFL player who had money now, but I wanted to save money to increase my spread. I wanted to make as much money as I could in the NFL and also through marketing and sponsorship opportunities. Then, I would work hard to keep my expenses down to create the largest spread possible. My discipline worked. This spread I created propelled my passive investing career in real estate. Again, it was all about my choices and what I valued.

SIDELINES

Is the Math Mathin'?

Basic financial literacy concepts are relatively easy to understand. This one is easy—the math has to be mathin'. This means that you must make more than you spend every month, and the larger the spread is between how much you make and how much you spend, the better off you will be.

- **In the black:** If your current TMI exercise showed that you have a spending average that is less than what you make, that's a good starting point.
- **In the red:** However, if your TMI number shows that you are spending as much or more than you are making every month, the math ain't mathin', and you need to make some changes.

If your solution is going to be, *I'll just cut out the lattes*, think again. Financial experts assert that by saying so long to Starbucks or nixing Netflix, you are on the road to saving money. But there is a much bigger picture here. This is about more than just cutting a coffee here and there.

Your financial situation will actually improve when you analyze and decrease your fixed expenses. The three that are crippling people are housing, debt, and transportation. So, let's dive deeper into each.

Housing

For most people, housing is the most significant expense. According to statistics from the U.S. Bureau of Labor Statistics, in 2022 American households spent an average of $24,298 per year on housing costs, which makes up 33.3 percent of their total average expenses.[4] Depending on where you live, that number can go higher or lower.

That doesn't mean that it isn't changeable. If you want to make a significant dent in your TMI, consider a possible move to somewhere that is less expensive. You might not want to, but remember, it's all about thinking like a future passive real estate investor.

For example, your monthly rent is currently $3,000, and you're living in a high-priced area of your community. It's a nice place, but your location could be preventing your success if it's stretching your budget. If you're not tied to that neighborhood for work or personal reasons, consider living in a more affordable one.

Let's say you find a new apartment a few towns away that costs only $2,000 a month. Boom. That $1,000 a month you saved will add up to a whopping $12,000 in just one year. If you make this move, by the end of the first year of studying the passive real estate industry, you will already have the money you need for a down payment on a property.

I purchased my first property with a friend with $12,000 of my own money while in the NFL, so I know it can be done.

If that same residence you used to rent also had common charges of $200 per month and your new place doesn't, that's another $2,400 per year you can add to the down payment or other expenses. I hope you understand the sentiment here. So many expenses come along with where you live, which is why it's often the best place to start when trying to significantly decrease your current TMI.

House Hacking

I know that not everyone wants to move to save money. If you can't or do not want to, there is still hope to reduce this pricey fixed expense. For

---

4   "Consumer Expenditures--2022," U.S. Bureau of Labor Statistics, September 8, 2023, https://www.bls.gov/news.release/cesan.nr0.htm.

example, if you own a home, you can use one of many clever house hacks to generate extra income. For instance, let's say you own a three-bedroom home with one unused bedroom. Can you rent it out? If your home has a finished basement, could you spruce it up and rent it while you still live there? Any rental income you receive can be saved to either pay down your mortgage balance or fund a down payment for an investment property.

House hacking is one of the best ways to reduce or eliminate housing expenses. If you rent out a space in your home, you may be able to live there for free, and that's putting 20 to 30 percent of your spending (the average for housing) back in your pocket.

If you are currently in the process of buying a home, consider a strategic move now and purchase a duplex. In a duplex, you live in one unit while you rent out the other. With this strategy you can own the duplex with a down payment as low as 3.5 percent. Then you can eventually move out, put a tenant in the unit you were staying in, and keep the property as a rental. You can go and buy the next property and house hack the exact same way, over and over. Or you can buy an affordable fixer-upper that you will live in while you renovate it. Then you can turn around, sell it for a profit, and move on to the next one a year later.

Depending on where you live, you can sell your current home, downsize to a less expensive place, or just move to a more affordable part of town. By selling your home, you could walk away with a healthy profit that you can then use to set up your real estate investing venture. Note that by selling, you may have to pay capital gains tax on the profits you make.

I understand that some of you may be in a place where none of these house hacking strategies are options you are willing to consider. As I write this, I am actually in that situation. My family and I love where we currently live, and we want this to be our long-term home, so moving isn't an option. I am also married with two young girls, so house hacking by allowing someone else to live with us is not a desire of mine. If you are at a similar place in your life, that is okay. Maybe reducing your living expenses isn't an option for you right now. That means you just have to make up for it somewhere else in your other fixed expenses.

Control the Debt; Don't Let It Control You

Many Americans have debt payments that amount to hundreds, and sometimes thousands, of dollars each month. Add that to your fixed expenses, and you're, in fact, decreasing your spread. To make it worse, many people only make the minimum monthly payments on their debts, so that amount is not getting much smaller as time goes on. Get out of that bad cycle by paying off debts that are dragging you down.

In 2023, the typical consumer paid $430 monthly toward credit card debt. Credit card debt is the main culprit to keeping you broke or slowing your progress on the journey to become a successful passive investor. Credit cards usually charge 20 percent or more in interest, and it's eating people alive. It's the worst kind of debt, and eliminating it should be priority number one.

On top of that, the average monthly student loan payment is an estimated $503, and the average borrower takes twenty years to repay all of it.

To reduce how much you're paying on either, start with a phone call to each lender. They might be able to reduce your monthly payment or interest rates, thereby saving you more money. However, if you reduce your monthly payments, you could be paying more in interest in the long run, so weigh your options.

As far as student loan debt, see if you can restructure your payments and/or come up with a plan to pay the debt off faster. Think about consolidating the loans, if that makes sense for you.

At the end of the day, start by evaluating where you have the most interest. Is this a credit card? A car loan? Your student loan? A 29 percent credit card bill is a priority, while a 5 percent car loan may not be.

Credit Scores

A credit score is a representation of your creditworthiness and indicates the likelihood of repaying debts based on your credit history. When you are buying real estate, your credit score plays a major role in the mortgage approval process. The higher your credit score, the greater the chance you have of getting approved for loans with favorable interest rates. The lower your credit score, the less chance you have of getting approved for a mortgage or, if you are approved, the higher your interest rate will likely be.

If your credit score is low, now is the time to try and improve it. You can do this by making sure you have your most recent credit report; check it for any errors. Then start paying off—or at least paying down—your debt. Try to pay more than your minimum monthly payment on your credit cards. More importantly, make sure you pay them on time. You can actually build credit by making minimal purchases on your credit cards, but make sure you pay those charges off at the end of every month.

Finally, keep your outstanding debt balances low in comparison to how much credit availability you have. For example, if you have a credit card with a $10,000 limit, try to keep your balance below $5,000. Do not max out your cards.

Transportation

Nowadays, the car you drive seems to be an extension of who you are, so many people are trying to make a statement with a flashy vehicle, whether it's something like a Tesla, Redeye Charger, G-wagen, or Rolls-Royce. For me, I can't lie. Growing up, I always wanted to drive either a Mercedes S 500 or a Range Rover, so trust me, I get it.

The problem is that the average monthly car payment for a new car is a whopping $729 and $528 for a used car. And if you finance or lease one of the cars I mentioned above, your car payment will be far more than that average. Be mindful of the decisions you make when obtaining a vehicle. I know a BMW is awesome to drive, but the higher monthly payment and higher insurance, registration, and maintenance costs could be crippling you. Is it all worth it just for the prestige of driving a Beamer? Or can you drive a more affordable Toyota for a little while?

Bigger Picture

When financial experts talk about saving money, it's always about cutting variable expenses. That helps, but it's the combination of both your variable and fixed expenses that's inhibiting you from increasing the spread and allowing you to thrive as a passive investor, so it's time to change your mentality and work on cutting both. Imagine the compound effect of reducing your fixed and variable expenses. For example, you move to a more affordable apartment (which saves $1,000 a month) and then restructure your monthly student loan payment (which saves $150 a month). You trade in your BMW for a Toyota (which saves $500 a month), cut your grocery and fast-food spending (which saves $200 a month), and decide that your monthly facial isn't valuable to you right now (which saves $150 a month).

In this example, you saved an impressive $2,000 per month by making just a few changes and phone calls. Now you have the option to go down two roads. You can either apply that money to decreasing your debt and strengthening your overall financial picture, or you can prep yourself to start investing passively.

If you decide to apply the money toward decreasing your debt, you could first pay off your high-interest monthly credit card debt. Once that is paid off, you then move the money you saved toward your student loans or an emergency fund. With this strategy, you have put yourself in a position to pay off debt or build an emergency fund much faster. These are all moves that help you earn the right to become an investor.

If you want to go down the investment road, you can save that $2,000 each month to put toward your first investment. After just one year, you would have saved $24,000 that you could use as a down payment for a property or lend to someone else going into investing. I hope you see the bigger picture now. There is no right or wrong decision here. It's all based on personal preference, but this gives you a glimpse of the power you gain from taking ownership of your expenses and control of your TMI. Simple yet effective moves like these can completely change your life in the short and long term.

Principles

One of my favorite quotes is from Ray Dalio, an American billionaire investor and hedge fund manager. In his popular book *Principles*, he wrote, "I learned that if you work hard and creatively, you can have just about anything you want, but not everything you want. Maturity is the ability to reject good alternatives to pursue even better ones."

Here is an example of how I interpret his words: Let's say your passion is cars. Dalio is saying that you can own cars if that is your desire (just about anything you want) and, instead, focus on reducing your rent or mortgage payment (but not everything you want). Here's another example: If your passion is travel and you want to spend your money on airfare and accommodations (just about anything you want), do it, but consider renting a less-fancy apartment because you're barely using the one you have anyway while you're jet-setting.

Dalio means that you can't be everything—a luxury house guy, a car guy, a travel guy, and a jewelry guy. If you try to have it all, you'll burn the money candle at both ends. As a result, reaching your financial goals of building an investment portfolio that works for this lifestyle becomes more challenging. Stay focused because one of the goals of this book is to show you how to obtain the financial means to pursue your goal of passive real estate investing.

Now you have a clearer view of your finances as well as a game plan for what changes to make, if changes are necessary. How exciting! Also, if you identified your current TMI, then you are farther ahead than most people who want to invest but don't know where to start. But having this information means nothing if you don't use it to make impactful changes and improvements.

Knowing your TMI and understanding your expenses is the base of this pyramid. Completing this step allows you to build an investment house on a solid foundation. If you skip it, you will be trying to create something on rocky footing, and it will be susceptible to failure. I'll say it one more time—your first goal should be to get your financial life in order and find extra dollars to reduce debt and save money, so you can then invest passively.

CHAPTER 4
INCREASE YOUR EARNING POTENTIAL

"Show me the money."

—Cuba Gooding Jr., *Jerry Maguire*

If you want to accelerate your journey to financial freedom, you must do more than just cut your expenses; you must increase your earning potential as well.

You can stop buying lattes, move to a cheaper apartment, buy a more affordable car, and eliminate streaming services that you don't use, but at some point, you are not going to be able to cut your expenses any further. Then what? There is no hard stop regarding how much you can earn, so it's essential to focus on what you're earning. If you are already working, put yourself in a position to squeeze the most out of that job.

There aren't any limitations on increasing your earning potential. You can earn as much as your heart desires, which is why this chapter is so powerful.

Through my football and business careers, I have identified four tried-and-true ways to increase earning potential, no matter what your profession is. And they are:

1. Get really good at what you currently do—they will have no choice but to pay you more.
2. Generate auxiliary income based on number one above, the fact that you are really good at what you do.

3. Add skills that attract more income.
4. Go where you will be paid more.

If you are serious about improving your financial life, funding retirement, being a successful real estate investor, or doing all of the above, lock in on pursuing at least one—if not all—of these things to increase your earnings potential.

Get Really Good at What You Do

In football, I always heard the phrase, "The cream rises to the top." This means that, with time, the people who are great at what they do will get recognized.

For me, I wanted to make as much money as I could when I was playing football. I set up my life, both on and off the field, to put me in that position. Without the proper training and mentality to play at my peak, I would be susceptible to injury, mistakes, or just outright poor performance that could get me sidelined.

Because of my desire to take advantage of my opportunity in the NFL to make as much as possible, I also chose to sacrifice during this time of my life. For example, during the season, I returned home after a very long day of work and would watch more film, study plays, stretch, and get in-home massages.

In the off-season, I loved to travel but I refused to take vacations that were longer than just a few days. That was because I didn't want to go for extended stretches of time without proper training. My mindset was that if I was on some island halfway across the world for two weeks, there would be another player in the States working his tail off to take my job. No way—I won't be outworked. I only drank alcohol occasionally in the off-season and not at all during football season and made sure to stretch, train, eat clean, and get at least eight hours of sleep a night. When our first daughter was born, my wife, Camille, handled the night shift so I could get my rest and be ready to perform the next day (thanks, Babe).

You have chosen to invest passively because you likely already have a job that you can't or don't want to leave. So, if you are going to continue to work there, why not make sure you are really good at what you're doing and earn as much money as possible doing it? I never understood people who were unhappy with how much money they made, but they didn't dig deep and become exceptional at whatever they did. Most likely, the money would then follow.

The problem is that the most addictive "drug" in the world is comfort. The amount of people who never reach their full potential because they got comfortable is alarming. Mike Tomlin, head coach of the Pittsburgh Steelers, is quoted as saying "Don't seek comfort." What he means by that is learn to love being uncomfortable because that is where you grow. So many people haven't even scratched the surface of what they are capable of accomplishing because they grow comfortable and complacent with the life, job, and career they have and forget how to seek or want more. I am sure you know at least one person who just clocks in and out every day and does just enough to get by. I even saw this in the NFL. Some players make some good money and then stop working as hard as they did when they first entered the league. They do enough to make sure they keep their job, but it's clear their heart isn't in it, and they are not working hard to improve. Those people are just wasting their time! If you have to be there anyway, why not work hard and be exceptional at your job to put yourself in a position to make more money? What are the things you can do to be the best you possibly can at whatever it is you do for a living? If you're comfortable, what's stopping you from doing those things? If you're stuck on what you should do, keep reading. Later I will give you some examples on how you can maximize your current job while you are building your real estate passive income.

Your priority should be to double down at your job so you can earn as much as possible, just like I did with football. When it was time to negotiate a new NFL contract, my work couldn't be denied. I had a great resume on the field, so I expected to be compensated accordingly. You should have that same mindset and apply it to your job, career, or business. When you are focused on being the absolute best you can be at something, your track record and expertise become your tools in a salary negotiation. My raise increased my earning potential and helped to increase my spread.

"But Devon, I don't want to work harder at my job. I want the real estate investments to work for me."

My answer to that is, *Do what you* have to *do now so you can do what you* want to *do later.*

There is no question that when you get further into your real estate journey, the investments will do the work and make the money for you. In the meantime, use your current job to leverage rewards. Make yourself so valuable to your company that it is obvious you should receive a promotion and raise. Put your current boss in a position where if they do not pay you what you deserve, then they will be at risk of losing you.

This is the easiest way to increase your spread so you can invest in real estate.

However, after time, if nothing has changed for you, then at least you will have created leverage for yourself to take to a place where you're more appreciated.

> *"The key to power is having options to give you leverage."*
>
> — Patrick Bet-David, YouTuber

Generate Auxiliary Income

Another great way to earn more is to find ways to generate auxiliary income, which is income that is related to what you already do. As a rookie, I played for the New York Giants, one of the best organizations in the NFL. I recognized that I had a great platform to leverage. I decided early on that I would do everything in my power to make as much money as possible off the field as I did on the field with marketing, sponsorship, and endorsement deals.

I knew there had to be opportunities that were too small for the big names on our team and that very few of the other guys were actively pursuing. Many players like me, who were not the superstars on the team, did not bother to pursue marketing opportunities because they thought that their names weren't big enough. "I'm gonna just focus on football," I would hear. My mindset was always all the big NFL names are focusing on football *and* pursuing off-the-field marketing and endorsement opportunities, so if they could do it, why couldn't I? I realized that this could become a huge advantage to me.

I took it upon myself to scoop up all those low- and mid-tier marketing opportunities. They added up well into six figures throughout my career. If I had never pursued those opportunities, it would have been lost money. And despite what everybody thought about it distracting me from football, it didn't. I could play at a high level year after year *and* make off-field money, which was the second way I increased my earning potential.

I hit a point while in the NFL where I was investing heavily in real estate but unable to find enough deals that made sense to me and would help me reach my financial goals. This led to my first auxiliary income within the real estate industry: private money lending. It was the perfect auxiliary income source because a) I was already in the real estate industry as an investor, b) I had built investor relationships, and c) I had some extra capital to invest. I could lend money to other investors and charge an interest rate ranging from 12 to 20 percent. These interest payments were additions to my income.

No matter what you do for a living, I am sure that you can find auxiliary sources of income, too.

For example, let's say you're an orthodontist who has a great reputation with your patients and your referral list is long. You earn a hefty annual salary, not an hourly salary. You work hard, but whether you see ten patients a day or one hundred patients a day, your paycheck is exactly the same. However, because of your current lifestyle and lingering debt, your salary still isn't enough to siphon away some money for investing. So how does a busy orthodontist increase earning potential? Auxiliary income for an orthodontist can come from writing books, medical journals, or giving speeches on the subject.

If you're a teacher and it's allowed, you might be able to make extra money tutoring in your subject area or selling your curricula to other teachers throughout the country. However, don't create a clothing line (unless you teach sewing) because the goal with auxiliary income is to make more money without going too far out of your current lane. Earning extra money doing what you're already doing is much easier than starting a brand-new side hustle from scratch.

Some of you reading this may feel you do not have the time or desire to generate auxiliary income, or you want to spend that extra time on being a passive real estate investor. If that is you, that's exactly why I have given multiple ways to increase your earnings. Taking on auxiliary income may not be for you. But I will say there may be some opportunities to make money that will not take significant time that already involves your day job. Make sure you are not missing a great opportunity.

The point is, do not unnecessarily complicate your life. Find ways to maximize your income based on what you already do for a living. Remember, your goal here is to increase your spread as much as you can, which will provide the funds you need for your real estate side hustle. For example, if you can easily make another $1,000 or more a month from auxiliary income, then you have brought in $12,000 in a year that can be put toward real estate investments.

Fill this in:

I can generate auxiliary income by doing _____

_____

Add Skills That Generate More Income

Another great way to increase your earning potential is to add skills to your resume.

Gone are the days when the only way, or even the best way, to prove yourself is with a college diploma. Recent studies suggest that it is track record and skill set that really distinguishes a person and puts them in a position to get a new job or promotion.

It truly does not matter what your profession or industry is, because there are always new skills you can learn that make you and your work unique and valuable, and directly impact the income you generate. Adding new skills can help you climb the corporate ladder, become a better salesperson, or skyrocket your six-figure business to seven figures.

Going into the 2018 football season, I hired a pass-rush coach to help me improve my skills so I could get more sacks. I added some great pass-rush moves to my toolbox, and I recorded seven sacks in each of the next two seasons, leading my team in both seasons.

This is how I was able to add skills in football, and I am sure there are ways you can add to your skill set within your job as well. Here's an example that I think is relevant today:

In 2024, ChatGPT is having an impact as a popular workplace tool. According to TechTarget's definition, ChatGPT is an artificial intelligence (AI) chatbot that uses natural language processing to create humanlike conversational dialogue. The language model can respond to questions and compose various written content, including articles, social media posts, essays, code, and emails.[5]

If you can find a way to incorporate ChatGPT into your business, you might become the person that is leading the charge within your company to onboard certain AI-backed software. That is an added skill

---

5   Amanda Hetler, "Definition ChatGPT," TechTarget, June 2024, https://www.techtarget.com/whatis/definition/ChatGPT.

set that warrants an increase in revenue. I recognize that certain industries have caps for certain skill sets but opportunities in others. For instance, a marketing coordinator may have limited earning potential, but a marketing professional with extensive data analysis skills may find better opportunities. How can you devote some time during your workday to build skills that will make you indispensable based on your current industry?

You are either getting better or getting worse; you never stay the same. Once you recognize that, you can really lock in on improving yourself, finding opportunities to earn more and ensuring that your skill set is always desirable in the marketplace. As a result, you will increase your spread, which creates the capital you need to passively invest in real estate. I hope by now you are seeing the value in earning more at your current job.

Go Where They Are Paying More

What if your salary is capped and you can't make more money at your job? What if you have added skills to your toolbox and have requested a raise or new position to no avail? It's unfortunate, but sometimes your best option is to go somewhere else, to a place where you will be respected, appreciated, valued and, most importantly, compensated appropriately.

In March 2020, I was in negotiations with the Detroit Lions for a contract extension. At the time, I was coming off my two best seasons in the NFL. I was also chosen as team captain and was nominated as a Walter Payton Man of The Year. With these accolades both on and off the field, I wanted my new contract to reflect what I had done.

Imagine my surprise when the Lions decided they did not want to pay me more and released me. Just a few days later, the Arizona Cardinals offered me the exact contract I wanted.

If you get to a place where you have performed well and are adding skills, but your company still refuses to provide additional compensation, you have a hard decision to make. Are you comfortable keeping your salary where it is and, instead, using one of the other ways to increase your earning potential? Or is it time to move on to another company and get paid what you're worth?

For example, if you are a public school teacher, can you find a job at a private school where they pay more? Can you relocate to a different public school district with a bigger budget? Does becoming a higher-paid principal interest you?

If you're a senior vice president making a healthy salary, you might be at the top of the ladder (except for the president), but you might be able to move laterally to another company or organization with more opportunities for raises and promotions.

Of course, these decisions depend on what you do for a living. I have friends in the tech world who switch jobs every few years when they hit a ceiling at their current workplace.

Spend some time studying your industry so you can make a rational decision about leaving. That way, if your boss tells you that they won't give you that raise or that there's no room for advancement, you can leverage your industry knowledge into working for a company that will.

Changing jobs isn't always easy, but if the new job pays you more, the outcome is having even more capital to invest in real estate. That may be your best option to reach your financial goals and build your real estate empire.

Simple but Hard

Too many times, I have seen people do the right thing, but if they do not see an immediate result, they stop. That is not how you increase your earning potential. You need to be in this for the long haul and have a strategic game plan behind what you are going to do.

I wish I could tell you there was a magical sauce that will automatically help you earn way more money, increase your spread, and build a real estate empire, but the truth is the answer is work. Work works.

I gave examples throughout this chapter to hopefully spark ideas of how you can increase your earning potential. Crack the code for your individual situation and figure out what you need to do and how. The solution is simple, but it's also hard work. If it was easy, everyone would be doing it. But those who succeed are the ones who roll up their sleeves and put in the work.

I will be the first one to acknowledge that my success as a professional football player was the linchpin in my investment journey. You may not think this applies to you because you're not an NFL player. But whether you're a teacher, small business owner, or a nine-to-five office worker, these principles can all be applied. I put my head down and worked hard at my job. That work started when I was only 8 years old and played peewee football. I reaped the financial rewards from the ages of 24 to 32, which then catapulted my real estate journey. Now get to work and go earn as much as you can.

An important thing to keep in mind is: The right action with the wrong amount of time can still fail.

When you start to do things to earn more money, you may not see the results overnight, but keep going. Think about it: You will get motivated from reading this chapter, so you go to work, have a great day, and expect a raise—but we both know it doesn't always work out that way.

One thing I learned during my football career is people who accomplish great things do ordinary things extraordinarily well and make a habit of it. If you want to stand out in your career, do ordinary things extraordinarily well, day in and day out, and at the right time, you will stand out and be financially compensated for it.

Now What?

With the last two chapters, if you've already done the work, you put yourself in a much better financial situation to kickstart your real estate investment journey. How powerful do you feel? *You* did that. Now it is time to take all that we have learned and practiced so far and set some financial benchmarks that will guide your investment journey and future.

CHAPTER 5

ACHIEVE BENCHMARKS

> *"Setting goals is the first step in turning the invisible into the visible, the anonymous into the known, the hidden into the seen."*

—Tony Robbins, author and business coach

When people ask me what real estate has done for me and how I think it can impact them, I always say that your ultimate goal should be to get to a place financially where you work because you want to, not because you have to.

When, not if, you get to that place, you will have put yourself in a financial position to continue working at a job you love without the added financial pressures, and you will have the option to walk away—all thanks to passive real estate income. That's a powerful feeling.

When I hung up my cleats from the NFL in 2023, I cannot explain how empowered I felt that I had built a successful real estate investment business over those last nine years, and I was now free to do whatever I wanted.

Benchmarks

In chapter 3, we identified your TMI number and learned the role that fixed and variable expenses have on that number. We then locked in on how to increase your spread by decreasing expenses and increasing your income. Now it's time to build on that work and set benchmarks for yourself that outline what you hope to accomplish.

Over the years, I did what you're doing now. I reviewed and trimmed my expenses and worked hard to increase my income, which increased my spread. Then, once I started earning passive income, I set financial benchmarks to help me create that freedom. For example, my first benchmark was to earn enough passive income to cover both my variable and fixed expenses. Once I achieved that, I would set the next benchmark even higher. And then higher again.

You are still a few chapters away from learning about your investment options and how to buy your first property, but I want to talk about it now because we are focusing on income and capital. And since we're already thinking about money and the importance it will play in your future, this is the best spot to talk about financial benchmarks.

In your life, financial benchmarks are the measuring sticks you use to compare your passive income to your TMI. This will dictate your investment risk tolerance, asset class (what type of investment is best for you), and strategies you need to implement to achieve each. For instance, if you have the desire to take your passive income to the moon (which is Benchmark 4) in the next ten years, then what you invest in and how aggressive you are will be a lot different from the person who just wants to have their passive income cover their TMI and is willing to work hard for fifteen years to get the job done.

To help you, I have created these four life-changing benchmarks to achieve (in this order):

- Benchmark 1: Passive Income = Fixed expenses
- Benchmark 2: Passive Income = TMI (fixed and variable)
- Benchmark 3: Passive Income = Double your TMI
- Benchmark 4: Passive Income = Abundance

Benchmark 1: Passive Income = Fixed Expenses

The first, most important benchmark to reach is earning enough passive income to be equal to or greater than your fixed expenses number from Chapter 3. Once you hit this benchmark, your boss could fire you, or your business could shut down tomorrow, and you would still have enough money coming in to cover all your necessities. You could keep your house and car, your debts would be paid, and your family would be taken care of.

To me, this is the most powerful benchmark because it gives you your first taste of financial independence away from your day job/career while providing economic stability for your household. Another great perk of reaching this benchmark is that if you happen to be in a job you do not like or you've asked for that raise and you're not getting it, you can quit and go after the job you really want and deserve without losing food on the table.

Many people get stuck in their job/career because they can't afford to stop working for a few months while they look for their next gig. This benchmark eliminates that. It takes you out of survival mode and moves you to an abundance mindset. It will provide you with peace of mind.

SIDELINES

From Survival to Purpose

While you're establishing your benchmarks, let's face which level of financial stability you are currently in and which level you want to strive to get to.

I break down financial stability into four levels:

- Survival
- Status
- Freedom
- Purpose

SURVIVAL

This is the level where you are simply just getting by. You are likely living paycheck to paycheck, have very little money saved up, and have few investments. This is where the math ain't mathin', and you are spending just as much or more than you make every month.

You're not alone. According to a LendingClub report, in 2023, a whopping 62 percent of adults said they were living paycheck to paycheck.[6]

STATUS

This is where you are starting to create some spread in your life (you're making a little more money each month than you're spending) and your innate desire is to buy and/or do the things you always wanted to buy and do. For example, in the NFL world, this is the player who signs his contract and buys a new car, house, and jewelry as soon as the money hits his bank account.

---

6   Jessica Dickler, "62% of Americans Are Still Living Paycheck to Paycheck, Making it 'The Main Financial Lifestyle,' Report Finds," CNBC, October 31, 2023, https://www.cnbc.com/2023/10/31/62percent-of-americans-still-live-paycheck-to-paycheck-amid-inflation.html

Unfortunately, what I have learned about this level is that as impressive as it is to get here, you won't stay here for long. You will likely start living outside of your means and fall back into the survival level. It's intoxicating to have extra money at this level, but if you don't know how to rein your spending in, you can be right back to where you were.

FREEDOM

This is the level where you have increased your spread even more and, as a result, start to leverage your new financial position. You begin to value your time and the ability to live life on your terms. At this level, you have the freedom to do what you want, when you want, and with whom you want, and you take great pride in that, as you should.

Many people seek to get to this level of financial prosperity and are completely comfortable staying here for the rest of their lives. However, it's obvious that most people aren't even close to achieving their own definition of financial freedom.

PURPOSE

This is the highest level of financial stability where your life becomes about more than just making money. Now you are making enough money that you can start to think about the impact you are having on future generations within your family, friends, community, and the world. Truthfully, not everyone has the desire or even the ability to reach this level, but I am sure you know some people who are at this level or on their way to it. They are no longer concerned with money at all because they have an excessive amount. Their main focus is now on their purpose.

Now, take a moment and ask yourself:

What level am I really at right now? _____

_____

What level do I desire to reach? _____

_____

I know that when I was growing up, the only financial stability level that I really desired to achieve was freedom. I have financial freedom now and worked hard to achieve it, and I thought I would be satisfied once I got here. But I have discovered a deeper purpose inside of me. It is to also help other people to change their lives financially. So that is why I wrote this book, to hopefully inspire and motivate you, but also to equip you with the tools you need to reach a higher level of financial stability and climb that pyramid to successful passive real estate investing. I would like to think it's safe to assume that if you are reading this book, you have the desire to go beyond the survival level so let's put that one aside for now.

It's important that you gain an understanding of what enough is for you. I know so many people who have more money than they ever imagined but are still unhappy. I think they have lost sight of what the real goal should be—not money but freedom, happiness, and purpose. You need to decide and understand which level gives you those feelings. That level is what you should be pursuing. Do not get caught up in just chasing more.

As you achieve your benchmarks, you will leave survival behind and walk the path to status, freedom, and ultimately purpose, if you desire.

The great thing about learning to invest passively in real estate is that after you do it once and develop the knowledge, skills, and capacity, nothing can stop you from repeating your success. Let's keep going.

Case Study of Benchmark 1

Jim earns $250,000 a year after taxes (rounded off for ease). His fixed monthly expenses are $5,000 and his variable monthly expenses are $7,000. Jim's TMI is $12,000, so he has an annual spread of $106,000. Here's how we got that number:

$$\$12,000 \text{ (TMI)} \times 12 \text{ months} = \$144,000$$
$$\$250,000 - \$144,000 = \$106,000$$

Jim wants to reach Benchmark 1, which means he needs to earn $5,000 per month from passive income ($60,000 annually) to cover his fixed expenses. He evaluates which investment options will give him that monthly return. After doing some research, he decides that purchasing ten single-family homes in the Midwest, where each property will net $500 a month, is the way to go. It took Jim two years to buy all ten properties, but he did it, and now he has $5,000 coming in passively every month.

 **SIDELINES**

If you're new to investing and think that this example of buying ten single-family homes out of the box is impossible for you, think again. There's an old saying, "There is only one way to eat an elephant, and that is one bite at a time." You can accomplish a goal like this, but you will only get there if you start with your first one.

Benchmark 2: Passive Income = TMI (Fixed and Variable)

If Benchmark 1 is the most important, then Benchmark 2 is the most popular. Why? This goal is the one that is synonymous with financial freedom.

I understood that if I could earn enough to cover my fixed expenses, I could certainly reach the next benchmark. That gave me the motivation to keep going.

Achieving this benchmark gives you the ability to sustain your lifestyle with or without your day job. In the investing community, there is a term FIRE, which means Financial Independence, Retire Early. Achieving this benchmark equals FIRE.

Case Study of Benchmark 2

Here's what this can look like, continuing with our case study of Jim. Remember Jim's TMI number is $12,000. He is now earning $5,000 from his investments, so he needs to figure out how to generate an additional $7,000 a month to cover his variable expenses. He decides that, over the next five years, he will buy ten more properties. He hopes to bring in an average of $500 in passive income each month per new property. In addition, he plans on raising the rent on the original ten homes. With both of these strategic moves, he should reach this benchmark of covering his TMI through passive income.

Benchmark 3: Passive Income = Double Your TMI

Benchmark 3 is growing your passive income numbers to cover your TMI twice over. I will be honest, not everyone has the desire to scale to this level. Many people are perfectly content with reaching Benchmark 2 and staying there for the rest of their lives. There is nothing wrong with that.

For those of you who want more, this benchmark is for you.

Do you want to buy an expensive luxury car? Travel first class or in private planes? Go on luxurious vacations? Help family members start businesses? Do you want to impact the next two, three, or four generations of your family? Everything you've done to reach Benchmarks 1 and 2 have already laid the groundwork for reaching this benchmark, and it's far easier than you may expect.

Case Study of Benchmark 3

Let's continue with Jim's journey. He now owns twenty properties in the Midwest that generate $12,000 a month ($144,000 a year). The beautiful thing is Jim has kept his job, so he maintains an annual spread of $106,000. That means that every year, Jim has an additional $250,000 ($144,000 in income from properties + $106,000 in spread from his day job = $250,000) to invest and work toward reaching Benchmark 3. I must note that this example hinges on Jim not using the income from his properties, because he still has his job. So, the $144,000 in income from properties increases his spread and expedites his investing journey.

In the meantime, the values of his properties are appreciating, and he is taking advantage of the tax benefits, depreciation, and debt paydown of owning real estate.

> **NOTE:** Debt paydown means that every month Jim is charging a tenant rent, and that rent is paying the mortgage. A portion of that mortgage payment goes to interest (which is a tax write-off) and the rest goes toward the principal balance. Every month the mortgage is getting paid down, which is increasing Jim's equity.

Also, Jim can continue to raise his rental rates a little every year so his passive income will steadily increase.

Jim has crunched numbers, and thanks to the passive income he is earning, he realized that the $250,000 per year he is saving is enough to buy eight modest single-family houses around $150,000 each in cash over the next five years. Over a five-year period, that adds up to $1,220,000. This will lower his risk by adding some no-debt properties to his portfolio and give him an even higher cash flow. Within five more years, he has reached Benchmark 3: Double your TMI.

He is expecting to net $1,500 a month per new property.

$$\$1,500 \times 8 = \$12,000 \text{ per month}$$

By the time he finishes the purchase of these additional eight properties, his portfolio will include twenty-eight properties that generate $24,000 or more each month for a passive income total of $288,000 each year. He accomplished this in less than fifteen years, while benefiting from all the extra cash flow. Powerful.

Benchmark 4: Passive Income = Abundance

After reaching Benchmarks 1, 2, and 3, some investors have no intentions of ever stopping. They love finding good deals and growing their portfolio. Benchmark 4 is all about taking your passive income to the level of pure abundance. What abundance means to me is that you have an overflow of passive income coming in. At this level, you may be bringing in three times, five times, or even ten times your TMI number.

I must note that there is nothing wrong with just achieving Benchmarks 1, 2, and 3. Do not feel like you have to go for this benchmark. With that said, there are certainly some of you who will not want to stop!

Reaching abundance is less about achieving an actual dollar amount, per se, and more about the fact that you are living in overflow and have reached income levels that only 1 percent of the 1 percent reach. Many people who have reached the to the moon income level have used their money to make large financial commitments to charities, start companies, and launch passion projects. What you do with this excess of capital is really up to you, but I encourage you to use some of it to make the world a better place.

Case Study of Benchmark 4

Jim's journey continues: Jim has now retired from his day job to spend time traveling the world while continuing to grow his real estate portfolio. He uses half of his passive income to sustain his lifestyle and the other half to continue buying properties with the goal of owning one hundred units one day. When you factor in all the benefits from owning nearly thirty properties he has now and all the ones he will buy in the future, Jim anticipates that his net worth and cash flow will double every seven years. In twenty years, Jim grew a portfolio of properties that took him from Benchmark 1 through 4 and, most importantly, he did it passively.

If you are thinking, *Man, twenty years is a long time to build this out*, I want you to put into perspective what you are comparing this to. Right now, you have a full-time job and probably contribute to a 401(k) and other retirement accounts, with the plan that eventually you will retire and live off these accounts. Get rich quick is not a realistic goal. Wealth building is a process that takes time, but it's important to note that throughout the twenty-year journey, Jim benefited financially every step of the way. He did not have to wait twenty years to reap the benefits. They just kept getting better.

Jim is an example of how you can build your retirement accounts with real estate investments and benefit along the way. By the time you retire, you will have built a portfolio that is generating a ton of passive income (depending on the benchmark you get to) and it has appreciated a ton over those years. This leaves you with a lot of options in your retirement years. Do you sell off some of your properties? Do you refinance the properties? Do you pay some of them off and pass them down to your kids? The moral of the story is building a robust portfolio may not be easy and it may take time, but in comparison to your alternative retirement accounts, it can be much shorter, and you will benefit along the way.

Compound Effect

Please understand that reaching every benchmark takes time and will depend on your situation. It won't happen in a week, a month, and probably not even a year. This is a marathon, not a sprint. However, if you stick to the fundamentals of increasing your spread and then reaching your benchmarks, I promise you will begin to see progress and pick up steam. It can be slow at first, like a snowball picking up speed and growing bigger as it goes downhill. Eventually, it will get so large that it's hard to stop.

While everyone's journey will be a little different, I think Jim's case study is a realistic example of how someone can build a real estate side hustle that takes very little of their time but has a lasting impact on their life. I hope you take the time to think about what benchmark levels you would like to reach and realize that you can build out a side hustle that will help you get there.

SECTION II CONCLUSION

Increasing Your Spread

Increasing your spread is not a one-and-done accomplishment. There is not a dollar figure you will get to when it will make sense to say, *Okay, I can stop now. I never have to worry about increasing my spread again.* Even if you finally quit your job and are only working on your side hustle passively, you still shouldn't stop trying to increase your spread. Life happens, so you need to commit to and revisit these concepts over and over.

Review Your TMI

Once I signed my contract with the Detroit Lions in 2018, I successfully increased my earnings, but my first child was on the way. Before Camryn was born, Camille and I knew what our TMI was and had our spending under control. But now we had a baby with the additional expenses of childcare, diapers, doctor appointments, clothes, and so on. My income went up, but so did our expenses. As a result, we needed to reassess our TMI regularly, otherwise my numbers would be inaccurate. Your life is fluid and things are always changing. Review your TMI at least one or two times each year to keep yourself on track.

With both your earnings and your TMI you need to:

- Monitor
- Tweak
- Reassess

Make this as normal for you to do as an annual medical checkup. Increasing Your Spread is the pyramid's foundation for a reason, so embody it.

Foundation Set

By following this blueprint so far, you have established a strong foundation for the pyramid. Now the real investment work begins. It's time to figure out what to do with the spread that you have created.

SECTION III
PREP FOR ACTION
LEARN AND GET ORGANIZED

Preparation is the key to success. It lays the groundwork for informed and decisive action.

Scale Up

Take Action

PREP FOR ACTION

Increase Your Spread

Your foundation is set! It's time to move up to Level 2—take action. Succeeding on this level is going to take consistent action on your part to learn four things:

- The language of real estate
- How to build your team
- How to create standard operating procedures
- The four passive investing vehicles

To complete this section effectively, you must first get into the right mindset. Before you read on, I need you to understand that this Level 2 work will need a minimum of a twelve-month commitment from you.

Don't feel overwhelmed by that amount of time. It does not mean you are slaving away on this material for forty hours a week for twelve months straight to learn it. Remember, this is a side hustle for you. It just means that once you finish reading the rest of the book, you will need to come back to this section and really study this material. The good news is that there aren't any tests. The true test of learning this material comes when you start buying investment properties. Do you understand what is happening? Can you spot a problem? Do you know what the terms of the deal are?

All you need to do to get started is to commit to the same amount of time you committed to in Section 1 of this book. That was when you reviewed your finances and calculated your TMI. Now you can use that time to learn how to take action.

As I already mentioned, I dedicated five hours a week to my real estate side hustle when I was in the NFL. In 2014, my first year before I purchased my first property, I spent those hours (which amounted to 260 hours in a year) focused on learning the same things you will learn about in this section. I am challenging you to do the same. If you're serious about being a successful passive real estate investor, do not skip coming back to this section. If you choose to skip the fundamentals, you are gambling with your financial future, not investing in it.

The best part of this section is that I will share with you what I already know works instead of leaving it up to you to figure it out for yourself. Having someone who has been in the trenches and can share what they have learned with you will put you in an even better position to succeed!

When I was in high school, I heard this quote from Abraham Lincoln that stuck with me:

"Give me six hours to chop down a tree, and I will spend the first four sharpening the axe."

This quote speaks to how important proper preparation is. Think about two men—one who uses a dull axe and is in a full sweat after four hours of chopping, but the tree still stands. Now you have another man who takes time to sharpen his axe and cuts the tree down in less than an hour without even breaking a sweat.

It may have looked like the man with the dull ax was ahead of the game because he got to work sooner, but it is clear that the man with the sharp axe was the real winner, chopping down the tree quicker because he knew that being prepared put him ahead.

This is the level of the pyramid where you sharpen your ax. Find two, five, or ten hours a week to learn this material because, in the next section, you will see how it applies to purchasing properties and, what you've been waiting for: making money. A year from now, you will see the fruits of your labor begin to blossom and be on your way to becoming a successful passive real estate investor!

Let's dive in!

CHAPTER 6

LEARN THE LANGUAGE OF REAL ESTATE

"Education is the passport to the future, for tomorrow belongs to those who prepare for it today."

—Malcolm X, revolutionist and activist

Believe it or not, I have some friends who do not watch professional football. When I show them an NFL playbook, they have serious trouble understanding it. They do not understand the complexities of the game and are shocked at how many plays are in it for the offense, defense, and special teams. Even true NFL fans who are dedicated to their teams and watch every game think they understand all the game's intricacies. But the truth is, there is no way they know how many details we, as players, need to know.

For example, I played outside linebacker on defense (I like hitting, not getting hit). When the opposing team's offense came out of their huddle, we were ready with a defensive play that had two parts. If the offense was set up in one formation, we ran one play. If they came out in a different formation, we ran a completely different play.

The tricky part was when the other team's play suddenly changed with a motion from someone on offense. For example, if their receiver shifted from one side of the football to the other, we had to quickly adjust and switch plays before the ball was hiked.

Because of these complexities, an NFL playbook has more than one hundred plays, each with variances. To the naked eye, it may look like hieroglyphics with the Xs and Os and route concepts and so on. It includes defensive terminologies, alignment names, etc., and we study for months to understand all the nuances, so that when that offense shifts, we can change our play in a second.

Believe it or not, learning the language of passive real estate is no different than when an NFL player learns their playbook! We need to learn how to speak the language of football, and you need to learn how to speak the language of real estate.

Twenty Core Terms

There will be many real estate terms you will learn as you become more versed in this industry. They will be tailored to the type of investments you will dive into. But to get you started, I've narrowed this chapter down to twenty core terms. This gives you a strong foundation to build on.

Do not even consider buying an investment property or making any real estate-related investments until you have a good grasp of these terms. It might seem like one big vocabulary lesson with a lot of math thrown in, but the language is vital to your success. I also tried to provide real-life examples with many of the terms, so you can see how they are applied in the industry.

Trust me that once you understand these terms, you will be able to hold conversations in a room full of investors and real estate professionals. You will also be able to make well-informed investment decisions because you a) understand how a deal will affect you financially and b) will not be taken advantage of.

Net Operating Income (NOI)

Net operating income reflects a property's ability to generate income after covering its day-to-day operational costs, such as maintenance, utilities, and property management. It's calculated by taking the total income generated by a property and deducting all the operating expenses, except for debt service (the amount needed to cover the mortgage every month) and taxes.

NOI Formula:
Total Income – Operating Expenses = NOI

The NOI will be a solid indicator of the building's profitability and can be a crucial factor when you evaluate its investment potential.

For example, the gross rent (rent before any expenses) on a single-family property for the year is $30,000 ($2,500 a month). The property's operating expenses add up to $10,000. The NOI would be $20,000.

$$\underset{\$30,000}{\textbf{(Total Income)}} - \underset{\$10,000}{\textbf{(Operating Expenses)}} = \textbf{\$20,000}$$

Now is $20,000 a good NOI for this property? In this case, yes. How did I figure that out? I like to make sure my operating expenses are less than 40 percent of the property's total income. I choose 40 percent because I have found that if the operating expenses on a property are 40 percent or higher, that property will have trouble cash flowing consistently. Now I have to determine what the percentage is of this property. In this case, having $30,000 in total income and $10,000 in operating expenses would mean that my percentage of operating expenses is 33 percent ($10,000 ÷ $30,000 × 100). That is under my threshold of 40 percent, so for me, this investment is a good one, purely based on the NOI.

However, it also depends on your initial investment amount and the projected return you had for this deal, but this is a good start.

Cash-on-Cash Return (CoC)

Cash-on-cash return assesses the performance of an investment. It gives you a clear picture of how much cash you're making relative to how much you invested. It's calculated by taking the investment's annual pre-tax cash flow and dividing it by the total cash investment.

CoC formula:

$$\underset{\textbf{Total Investment Amount)}}{\textbf{(Net income ÷}} \times \textbf{100} = \underset{\textbf{percentage}}{\textbf{CoC as a}}$$

For example, if you invested $50,000 in a property and the cash flow you pocketed was $5,000 in a year, then that would be a CoC return of 10 percent ($5,000 ÷ $50,000 = .1 × 100 = 10%).

Capitalization Rate

Better known as the cap rate, this gauges the rate of return on an investment property you can expect from its income. It is calculated by dividing the property's net operating income by its current market value or acquisition cost (how much a property is purchased for). A higher cap rate suggests a higher potential return. Still, you must consider other factors like risk, location, and market conditions before investing in a property solely on its cap rate.

$$\text{Cap Rate} = \frac{\text{Net Operating Income}}{} \div \frac{\text{Current Market Value OR Purchase Price}}{} \times 100$$

For example, if the NOI on a duplex is $20,000 and you bought the property for $300,000, the cap rate would be 6.6 percent. $20,000 ÷ $300,000 = .05 × 100 = 5%. Whether a 6.6 percent cap rate is a good return or not is based largely on a) the specific market of the property and b) the expected returns you have set for yourself. For example, I know some investors who won't look at a property that does not hit at least a 6 percent cap rate, while other investors will jump on a property with a 5 percent cap rate, so you must determine what is a good deal to you.

Return on Investment (ROI)

Return on investment evaluates the profitability of your investment, combining both cash flow and appreciation (how much the value of a property has increased). It's calculated by dividing the gain (profit) from the investment, including the cash-on-cash return and the appreciation of the property, by the initial purchase price, then multiplying it by 100 to express it as a percentage.

ROI = Gain from Investment ÷ Cost of Investment × 100

ROI assesses how effectively your money is being utilized and the financial return you're getting compared to how much you initially invested into the property. Many people confuse CoC with ROI. CoC focuses specifically on the cash income you earn relative to how much cash you invest. However, ROI considers the total return, including any appreciation in the property value.

Let's assume that on a single-family property you purchased and renovated for $350,000, you had a CoC return of $10,000 for the year. But because you renovated the property, its value has increased to $420,000. Your ROI is now 22 percent.

$10,000 of cash flow + **$70,000 of appreciation** ÷ **$350,000 of the all-in price** = **.22 × 100 = 22%**

Internal Rate of Return (IRR)

By now, you have learned a few core terms that focus on return on investment, but they all differ a little from each other. The internal rate of return (IRR) measures the return of an investment, but it also considers the time value of money. In other words, it accounts for the entire cash flow timeline of the investment, which offers a holistic view of profitability.

This is explained better with an example. Let's say you invested $100,000, and in one year, you receive your $100,000 back plus an additional $100,000 of profit for a total of $200,000. In this case, calculating your IRR is simple—it's a 100 percent IRR because you doubled your money in one year. But if you invested $100,000 and it took five years to get the exact same $100,000 of profit, then your return is 18.92 percent.

You received the exact same amount of money in both scenarios, but because the second scenario took five years instead of one, your IRR decreased by over 80 percent. Calculating IRR is not something you can do on your own, like you can with the other return metrics. It needs to be input into an IRR calculator or spreadsheet.

The IRR helps investors gauge how long they should hold on to an investment before the return starts to decrease. For instance, two investors buy triplexes that they plan to renovate and sell. One investor takes six months to renovate and sell while the other one takes two years. The investor who sells in six months will have a higher IRR return (assuming they sell it for the same price).

Fair Market Value (FMV)

Fair market value is a crucial concept in real estate transactions as it establishes a reasonable and unbiased value of your property. It is the price that the property would likely sell for in an open and competitive market. Factors that determine its value include comparable sales, the property's condition and location, and current market conditions.

After Repair Value (ARV)

After repair value is just like what it sounds. It estimates a property's potential value after it has undergone necessary renovations or repairs. This is a key metric, especially if you want to be a fix-and-flip real estate investor. The ARV considers the current condition of the property, the cost of repairs or renovations, and the expected increase in the property's value after improvements. Investors often use ARV to evaluate whether a property has the potential for a profitable resale or refinance after making the enhancements.

Theoretically, you would think that if you renovate any part of a property, the renovation should increase its value. Unfortunately, that's not always the case. For instance, one of your properties may need a new roof. That is a renovation and repair, but it doesn't increase the property value. Why? A buyer expects the roof to be in good shape. They will not pay extra just because the roof is brand new. On the other hand, a full kitchen rehab in a nice neighborhood will increase the value of the home. A buyer may pay $10,000 over the asking price because they love the new kitchen that has an island and is open to the living room area.

Market Rent

Market rent refers to the rental rate that a property will likely command in the open market. It's determined by analyzing comparable rental properties in the area and considers such factors as location, property features, and overall supply and demand. It helps in setting a competitive and fair rental price that aligns with the current state of the local real estate market.

For example, you buy a rental property and charge your tenant $1,000 monthly to live there. However, thanks to analyzing comparable rental areas in the area, you learn that this property would command a rate of $1,200 per month.

Comparative Market Analysis (CMA)

A comparative market analysis is the evaluation of the current market value of a property by comparing it to similar properties (comparables or "comps") in the same area that have recently been sold, are currently on the market, or were listed but didn't sell. Real estate agents often use CMAs to help sellers determine what an appropriate listing price for their property would be or to assist buyers in making informed offers.

For example, you may find that when you do your research, the property you want to buy is listed for $400,000, but comps show that other area properties are selling for only $350,000. As a result, you might lower your offer to purchase it, depending on other factors.

Underwriting

Underwriting is the process of evaluating the potential risk and return of any investment. This is done by researching information relevant to the property you are buying and then running the potential returns the property will earn against how much you invested. Some of the information you will be gathering during your due diligence is comparable sales in the neighborhood, rent projections, confirming property taxes, condition of the property, how long the current owner has owned it, rough estimates on any repairs or renovations needed, inspection report results, interest rate your lender will offer, the kind of insurance the property will need, and the potential ARV of the property. You will then use all this information to create your pro forma (a projection of what you expect the return on the investment will be).

Learning how to underwrite your properties effectively may be the single most important skill you will pick up as a passive real estate investor. Underwriting used to take weeks, but thanks to the internet, and real estate investment software and apps, you can obtain all the information you need—such as the ROI, CoC, cap rate, and more—in a matter of hours or even minutes. In a short period of time, you can underwrite your deals and assess whether a potential property is a good or bad investment.

Loan to Value (LTV)

Loan to value is commonly used in mortgage lending and represents the percentage of the purchase price that you financed through a lender. LTV is a crucial factor in mortgage underwriting because it determines if you will be approved for a loan, what interest rate you may receive, and if you will require any mortgage insurance.

LTV is expressed as a percentage and is calculated using the formula:

$$\text{(Loan Amount} \div \text{Purchase Price or Appraised Value)} \times 100 = \text{LTV}$$

Let's say you buy a home for $400,000 and put 25 percent down ($100,000) with a conventional loan to cover the $300,000. The property was appraised for $450,000.

To calculate the loan to value, you need to take your loan amount of $300,000 ($400,000 purchase − $100,000 down payment = $300,000) and divide that by $450,000 (the appraised value) which equals .66. Then multiply .66 × 100 to get a 66 percent LTV. Whether a certain LTV is good or bad is completely dependent on what your goals and risk tolerance are.

SIDELINES

The reason LTV impacts risk tolerance is the more money you have borrowed on a property, the more inherently risky it is because you now have a higher mortgage to pay. In the case above, if you have an LTV of 90 percent instead of 66 percent, your mortgage payments will be higher, and it may be harder to be cash flow positive from the rent collection. Some investors do not mind this extra risk because they think they are mitigating risk by not having as much money in the deal. Your viewpoint on what is high or low risk and how to mitigate that is extremely personal.

For instance, I once had an LTV of 25 percent across my entire real estate portfolio. As I acquired more properties, I planned to keep my portfolio LTV below 50 percent. While I think that is great, an investor with higher appetite for risk might say that I am being far too conservative, and I should take more advantage of the equity to scale and buy more. But you need to determine what LTV makes sense for you. That will come in time.

Many lenders have a maximum LTV that they will give out to investors. For instance, my lender now will lend me up to 80 percent LTV, which means I need to come up with 20 percent of the purchase price.

Capital Expenditures (CapEx)

CapEx refers to any long-term investments made to maintain, upgrade, or improve a property's overall value. These expenditures go beyond routine repairs and day-to-day operating costs that keep the property in its current condition. It includes major renovations, such as replacing a roof or HVAC system, fixing foundation issues, replacing single-pane windows with double-pane windows, or any improvement that extends the property's useful life.

I purchased a six-unit property that needed a full rehab. My contractor took the inside of the building all the way down to its studs. They put in new piping, flooring, walls, cabinets, and outlets. I categorized this entire rehab project as a CapEx expense. Understanding and budgeting for CapEx is crucial for property owners and investors to ensure the property's sustained value and plan for long-term financial stability.

Repair and Maintenance (R&M)

Repair and maintenance refers to ongoing efforts and actions to keep a property in good working condition, prevent deterioration, and address any wear and tear. This includes fixing specific issues or damages that affect the functionality or safety of the property—for example, fixing a leaky roof, repairing a broken window, or addressing plumbing issues. Other examples include regular cleaning, landscaping, painting, and servicing HVAC systems. Property owners and managers typically allocate funds for these purposes. R&M is considered operational and is usually less expensive in comparison to CapEx expenses.

Vacancy Rate

A property's vacancy rate provides insight into the supply and demand dynamics of the rental market where the property is located. It does this by measuring the proportion of rental units or properties that are currently unoccupied or available for rent and dividing it by the total number of units that the property has. It's typically expressed as a percentage—the lower the better.

For example, if you own a single-family property and it's vacant, then you have a 100 percent vacancy rate. If you own a multifamily building with one hundred units and ten of them are vacant, the vacancy rate is 10 percent. A higher vacancy rate may suggest oversupply or that economic factors are affecting demand, while a lower vacancy rate could indicate a highly sought-after rental market.

1031 Exchange

A 1031 exchange is a strategy that allows you, the investor, to sell a property and reinvest the proceeds into another property of equal or greater value without immediate tax consequences. The "1031" refers to Section 1031 of the Internal Revenue Code, which outlines the rules for this type of exchange. There are three key points of a 1031 exchange:

1. **Like-kind property:** The properties involved must be of like kind, but this doesn't mean identical. It generally refers to the nature or character of the property, not its quality or grade. For example, if you sell a small single-family home, you can 1031 exchange into a bigger single-family home.

2. **Timing:** There are strict timelines you must follow. The replacement property must be identified within forty-five days of selling the relinquished property, and the exchange must be completed within 180 days.

3. **Qualified intermediary:** To ensure this exchange qualifies for a tax deferral, a qualified intermediary (this individual makes sure

everything happens according to the IRS guidelines) facilitates the process and holds the funds between the sale and purchase. This exchange allows investors to defer capital gains taxes (taxes you pay on the money you made from the sale of the property) that would normally be triggered by the sale of an investment property.

Equity

Equity represents the ownership interest that an owner holds in their property. In simple terms, it's the portion of the property that you, as the owner, truly own outright.

Equity Formula:

$$\text{Property's Market Value} - \text{Total Liabilities (mortgages and loans)} = \text{Equity}$$

Positive equity is when the property's value exceeds the debts, while negative equity (or being "underwater") happens when debts surpass the property's value. For example, if a property you own is worth $500,000 and your outstanding mortgage on it is $200,000, your positive equity is $300,000.

Closing Costs

Closing costs are the fees and expenses charged during the final stages (closing or settlement) of a property transaction when ownership is transferred from seller to buyer. How much these cost depends on the type of property, its location, and the terms of the mortgage.

Common closing costs include:

- **Loan origination fees:** charges from the lender for processing the loan.
- **Title insurance:** protects the buyer and lender against issues with the property's title.
- **Appraisal fees:** the cost of assessing the property's value.
- **Escrow fees:** fees for managing funds and documents during the transaction.
- **Home inspection costs:** the cost a home inspector charges if the buyer purchases a home inspection.
- **Recording fees:** charges for recording the sale of the property with local authorities.

Whether you come into the transaction as the buyer or the seller, it's important to know what the closing costs are ahead of time. If you are the buyer, you should factor them into your budget.

Settlement Statement

This document outlines the costs and fees associated with a real estate transaction. It is created by the title company at the closing of the property and breaks down every fee and who is getting paid. At times I have had to request the settlement statement, so if you do not automatically get one, make sure you ask for it.

Title Company and Escrow Agent

A title company handles the title search of a property, which confirms the property's ownership history. Title companies also handle all the documentation of a purchase to ensure a clean transfer of ownership.

An escrow agent is a neutral third party who holds the funds and documents until the real estate transaction is complete. I put the title company and escrow together because, in most purchases, the title company acts as the escrow agent.

Deed

This is a legal document that transfers ownership of a property from the seller to the buyer.

Two Main Asset Classes

You have a basic understanding of twenty core terms, many of which are on the financial side of investing. Now let's talk about the two main asset classes—or types of properties—that you can invest in. Both asset classes have their own risk and return profile for investing, and the right choice depends on what your investment goals are, your risk tolerance, and the current market conditions.

1. **Asset class 1—residential real estate**: Residential means just what it sounds like: where people reside or live. Your real estate investing options in this asset class are single-family homes, condominiums, townhouses, and small multifamily properties up to four units.

2. **Asset class 2—commercial real estate**: Commercial real estate encompasses properties that are used for business or

income-generating purposes. Many different asset classes fit under commercial real estate but some of the most common are multifamily buildings (apartments), office buildings, industrial buildings, hospitality (hotels/resorts), healthcare buildings, and storage facilities. Just about every building you see that is not a residential home is some type of commercial real estate.

In addition to the obvious difference between residential and commercial real estate—home and business—there are three other differences to consider:

1. **Valuation**: This is the worth of the property you're investing in. How it's calculated depends on what type of property you own:
   - **Residential:** The valuation of a residential property, such as a single-family home or condominium, is based on comparable sales in the neighborhood and considers factors like size, location, and condition.
   - **Commercial:** The valuation of a commercial property, such as a mall or a multifamily property, is based on its income potential.

2. **Financing**:
   - **Residential:** If you are purchasing a home, it often involves applying for a traditional mortgage with lower interest rates and a thirty-year fixed loan.
   - **Commercial:** Financing is often more complex, and terms of a loan are heavily influenced by the property's income and purpose. These loan interest rates are typically higher than residential ones, and the loan lengths are much shorter.

3. **Regulations**: The rules that come along with owning an asset are based on property type and location.
   - **Residential**: Regulations are standardized and focused on ensuring the safety of the property for residents. Examples of residential regulations could be the number of smoke detectors you are required to install in a house, guidelines on plumbing to maintain sanitation, and standards for electrical wiring throughout the house.
   - **Commercial**: Regulations vary widely and depend on the property type and its use. Zoning laws, building codes, and environmental regulations all play a significant role in what these regulations are. An example is compliance with the American Disability Act (ADA), which sets requirements for how many handicap parking spots your building needs to provide.

In addition to these two main asset classes, there are other opportunities to make money in real estate.

- **Financing:** If you have capital or access to capital, you can provide funds for real estate deals, through traditional lending, private loans, or other financing methods.
- **Syndications:** This is a strategy where multiple investors pull their capital and expertise together to invest in larger real estate projects.

I have found that single-family/small multifamily properties, syndications, private money lending, and commercial real estate are great real estate side hustles and the ones that I have used most. Keep in mind that once you determine which asset class and/or strategy you are interested in, you will learn even more terminologies that are specific to that interest.

 **SIDELINES** _ _ _ _ _ _ _ _ _ _ _

Property Classes

It's common practice to classify the quality and location of a property with an A–D classification. Here is a breakdown of what each means:

- **Class A**: These properties are typically in prime locations that have high demand. They are newer or recently renovated with modern amenities and features. Class A properties attract high-income tenants and usually command premium rents. They generally have lower maintenance costs and fewer management issues.
- **Class B**: Class B properties are well-maintained but may be older or less modern than Class A properties. They are located in stable or transitioning neighborhoods. Class B properties offer good rental income potential at more moderate rents compared to Class A. These properties may require some updates or renovations to maximize their value.
- **Class C**: Class C properties are typically older, with some level of deferred maintenance. They are located in areas that may have more economic challenges or a lower demand. Class C properties offer lower rental rates but can provide higher cash flow due to lower purchase prices. These properties often require more ongoing maintenance and management.
- **Class D**: Class D properties are often in distressed or highly challenging locations. They may require significant renovations or even complete redevelopment. Class D properties generally have the lowest

rents and attract tenants with limited financial means. Investing in Class D properties carries higher risk but can potentially offer higher returns if successfully revitalized.

These classifications help investors determine the type of property and location they want to invest in. For example, when I started out, I was buying Class C properties that cash flowed well. Now I prefer to buy Class B properties that are of higher quality and in better locations. The class of property you buy should be based on your own goals and risk tolerance. If you are looking for a high cash return and are willing to take on some risk, then either Class C or D may be something to consider. If you are looking for stability and long-term growth, Class A or B properties may be the way to go.

It's important to note that these classes are for single-family and commercial real estate. For example, a hotel (or any commercial property) can be an A class property in a great location or a C class property in a more challenging location.

The Application of What You're Learning

In addition to helping you make educated decisions on the best investments for you, learning the language can also prevent you from being taken advantage of. I know this from personal experience. I was six years into my own investment journey, and it *still* happened to me. I had been investing since 2014, but in 2020 I had yet to deal with a rehab project. I had stayed away from them because I thought they would take up too much of my time, and I didn't know enough about the process.

However, when I wanted a home for my own family, I decided to buy a fixer-upper and do a full remodel instead of buying a top-dollar, brand-new place. My wife and I found a contractor who said all the right things to us:

"We can get this project done in four months or less."

"I have all the subs hungry and ready to go."

"I have contacts who can get wholesale pricing on cabinets, countertops, and flooring, so I can come in under budget."

"This will be easy for me! I have done much larger projects than this!"

Hearing him talk like this excited us, and I was committed to the work he could do.

I consider myself a smart and educated man, but even the most knowledgeable people make mistakes, and I made a big one. I didn't get any of this in writing. I trusted him, but halfway through the project, I caught on that he was completely screwing us over. Yes, he had given me a budget and a timeline, but a project that was supposed to take only four months ended up taking nine. He added expense after expense to the bill.

By the time I figured all of this out, I had two options: 1) let him finish the job, even though it was taking longer and costing more, or 2) start from scratch trying to find a contractor who would take over the job.

We were ready to move into our home and decided that finding someone new would likely push us back months, so I felt trapped and stuck it out with him.

At the time, I considered myself a savvy investor, but I didn't know enough about the construction side of real estate investing, and this contractor knew that without that signed contract, he could—and did—take advantage of me. If I had learned more about working with a contractor, I would have learned more about signed contracts and this would not have happened. Lesson learned.

I want to keep you from making the same mistakes in your journey. I am much more experienced and knowledgeable about the industry now, so I will pass this on to you.

And finally, the best way to learn the language is by *doing*! Don't get stuck in the learning phase. Put this all to use by talking to investors and real estate agents and asking questions or talking about the market. Call a general partner and ask questions about syndications. Use these conversations to see how much you understand.

 **SIDELINES** _ _ _ _ _ _ _ _ _ _ _

Keep Learning

It's time to expand your knowledge even further. You already have a lot to digest, but it's okay to be a sponge right now and try to absorb as much real estate investing info as you can.

- **Podcasts/YouTube**: I challenge you to choose three podcasts about real estate investing that you commit to listening to every week. Right now, my top three are *BiggerPockets On The Market Podcast*, *Real Estate Investing with Coach Carson*, and *The Weekly Juice Podcast*. The knowledge you will gain from these experts is amazing. If you prefer visual media, each of these podcasts can also be found on YouTube.

- **Books**: Additionally, I challenge you to read at least six real estate books in the next year in addition to mine. I recommend:
  - *The Lifestyle Investor: The 10 Commandments of Cash Flow Investing for Passive Income and Financial Freedom* by Justin Donald
  - *Lend to Live: Earn Hassle-Free Passive Income in Real Estate with Private Money Lending* by Alex Breshears and Beth Johnson
  - *The Hands-Off Investor: An Insider's Guide to Investing in Passive Real Estate Syndications* by Brian Burke
  - *The Small and Mighty Real Estate Investor: How to Reach Financial Freedom with Fewer Rental Properties* by Chad Carson
  - *Long-Distance Real Estate Investing: How to Buy, Rehab, and Manage Out-of-State Rental Properties* by David Greene
  - *The E-Myth Revisited: Why Most Small Business Don't Work and What to Do About It* by Michael Gerber
- **Social media**: If I am going to be on social media, I want to spend time learning and picking up good nuggets of real estate information. It's a safe bet that you also spend a decent amount of time on social media. So use it to follow, learn, and interact with people in the real estate space. My entire Instagram and Twitter feeds are about real estate now because I follow so many pros. You'd be surprised at how much I have learned by following other investors over the years. I also use social media to interact with these investors and have built many offline relationships that have directly impacted my investing success.
- **Events**: Tap into your local real estate market and find out where their industry meetups are. This is an easy way to meet like-minded people and professionals who can help you achieve your goals. Then expand beyond your local horizons and attend the bigger real estate conferences, such as BPCON (BiggerPockets hosts a mutliday real estate investment conference, and you can learn more about it at www.BiggerPockets.com/events) or Limitless (the financial freedom expo). Conferences like these are an easy way to learn from and meet other real estate experts.

This is your playbook. Study it often. When I was playing football, I had to know my playbook so well that when the coach called a play, I knew exactly what I needed to do, what changes would happen if the offense changed their formation, and so on. That is how well you need to understand your real estate playbook. Just keep in mind though that it's not good enough to be able to spit out definitions. You must be able to hold a conversation about, for example, CoC, and be able to calculate it (using a calculator) on the fly. When you get to this point, you know you are ready for the next step—building out your team.

CHAPTER 7

BUILD YOUR TEAM

"All-stars like working with all-stars."

—Devon Kennard, author and former NFL player

Learning the language and building your team can overlap. While I was reading books on real estate, going to events, and following experts on social media, if I ever thought someone could potentially become a mentor, partner, or part of my team, I would look up their social media, phone number, or email and reach out.

This happened in 2018 when I had just signed a new contract with the Detroit Lions—increasing my spread—and now had more money to invest. I already owned six properties in Ohio and was a limited partner in ten different syndications (which we will discuss in a later chapter). Still, I didn't quite know what direction to go next.

I was listening to an episode of the *BiggerPockets Real Estate Podcast*, hoping to gain more knowledge and get clarity on my next move. The guest on that episode was named Nathan, who was successfully flipping hundreds of homes each year in his Kansas City market. He explained his process from start to finish; once he was done fixing his properties, he sold them to other investors who wanted to buy and hold in his market.

As he was talking, Nathan mentioned that he had a team of wholesalers and agents who helped him find great off-market deals, multiple contractor crews to manage all his flips, property management companies he partnered with to manage the properties, and local and national lenders to help fund his deals. While listening, I thought to myself, *Wow, this dude is in a great market to invest in and has a team in place.* I did some research, and, at the time, you could buy turnkey properties in Kansas City for less than $100,000. I wanted to invest in this market, so I sent Nathan a direct message on Facebook introducing myself and expressing interest in investing in his market. We hit it off and began to foster a great relationship. He started to send me deals and shared specific market information with me. He connected me to his entire team, which I was then able to adopt as my team. Then, I invested in six properties in the Kansas City market.

The Lesson: I was listening to the BiggerPockets podcast to learn more, but in fact, I identified a new market that I could invest in, made a connection, and found a team to work with me in Kansas City. This all came from listening to one episode.

I am not saying that if you reach out to someone, you will have the same results that I did—although you could—but I am saying that building a team is not nearly as difficult as you might think. It could start with just a simple phone call or email. That's because all-stars like working with all-stars.

NBA legends like LeBron James and Kevin Durant are perfect examples of this. All-stars like working with all stars because, ultimately, they all want to win, and they understand that if they work together, they can achieve something special. LeBron left the Cleveland Cavaliers to play with fellow NBA superstar Dwyane Wade and the Miami Heat. Kevin Durant left the Oklahoma City Thunder to join Stephen Curry and the Golden State Warriors. During their four seasons together, LeBron and Dwyane won two NBA finals, four NBA Eastern Conference championships, and the Southeast division four times. Kevin and Stephen went on to win two NBA titles in three trips to the finals.

You don't need to be a professional athlete to accomplish something similar. All you need to do is identify a real estate all-star in the market you wish to invest in. To find one, it ultimately comes down to taking advantage of the resources you have at your disposal: social media, events, books, podcasts, and last, but certainly not least, recommendations from other professionals.

Identifying a real estate all-star is just the first step. You must position yourself as an all-star passive investor that is worth working with. Think about it: if Dwyane Wade wasn't a proven all-star himself, would Lebron have been interested in joining him?

So, what does a passive investor all-star look like? They have a great understanding of real estate, are easy to work with, have access to capital that they are ready to deploy, have a clear idea of what they are looking for, can execute and close deals, and so on. Once you get to the point in your journey where you can position yourself as an all-star, it will be much easier to attract other all-stars.

That's what happened to me. After reaching out to Nathan, the podcast guest, I had to foster that relationship and show that I was knowledgeable, serious, and ready to take action. One way I could prove this was by taking a trip out to Kansas City. This served two purposes:

1. To meet and interact with him and his team directly. I like meeting the people I will be working with so I can get a better gauge of character and make sure I can envision myself with them.

2. Giving them the chance to meet me. I want them to see that I am serious about investing in their market. Nothing shows that more than an in-person visit. After the trip, I had full access to Nathan's team and started purchasing properties.

Core Four

The bread-and-butter team members that every investor needs to have on their team is what I call my Core Four (I am pretty sure I originally heard this term from a BiggerPockets episode as well):

1. Deal Finder
2. Contractor
3. Property Manager
4. Lender

Who should you find first? Without a doubt, it's the deal finder! A common quote in the real estate world is: "You make your money on the buy," and the deal finder is the person who helps you find discounted properties. The rest of your team is, in large part, dependent on the investment vehicle you choose.

Deal Finder

Deal finders either have experience as an investor or regularly work with investors. They can be a:

- **Wholesaler:** Someone who scouts for distressed or undervalued properties off the market and is not licensed.

- **Agent:** A licensed real estate professional who facilitates the buying, selling, or renting of real estate on and off the market.[7]
- **Broker:** Like agents, brokers are licensed, but they have additional education and experience requirements and can either work independently as an agent or be the lead in their brokerage firm.
- **Real estate investor:** Another investor who finds on- and off-market deals through their network.

Nathan was my deal finder—more specifically, a turnkey provider for investors like me. A turnkey provider is someone who offers a fully packaged property from acquisition to renovation to property management. He became a one-stop shop and connected me with his whole team. With these deals, I didn't need a lender because I bought the properties in cash.

The key here is that these people are pros at finding and evaluating opportunities.

What Are the Qualifications of an All-Star Deal Finder?

1. **They have been in business for a while.** Ask them how long they have been a wholesaler/agent/broker/investor. While newbies can positively impact the industry, someone who has been in the trenches for at least a few years brings this experience to the table.
2. **They know their market.** When I talked with Nathan about the Kansas City market, he was jam-packed with knowledge about the area. Once you start talking to someone in an asset class that you want to invest in, you can tell whether they know that market.
3. **They have a successful track record.** When it comes to working with deal finders, my general guideline is to work with one who has been doing it for at least three years and has been part of multiple transactions within the last twelve months. For me, the more experience, the better. Ask if they will give you references of some investors they have worked with.
4. **They have worked with two or more investors.** Working with just one is fine, but I like seeing that they can work well with others and have proven to do so in the past.

---

7   Having an investor-friendly agent on your team is the most important for investors getting started. You can use the BiggerPockets Agent Finder to quickly find local, investor-friendly real estate agents who can help you find, analyze, and close the best deal at www.BiggerPockets.com/bookagent.

5. **They prioritize you and your needs.** Do they have the bandwidth to help find your properties? I always fear working with an extremely experienced deal finder because I wonder if they have time to send me deals. This is a question you just have to ask straight up.
6. **They know how to underwrite deals.** You will be surprised how many deal finders (especially real estate agents) will promote themselves as investor-friendly but have no idea how to underwrite a deal. This is an automatic red flag that they are not an all-star deal finder.
7. **They built out a successful team.** They know others in their market who are great at what they do.

If a deal finder meets these guidelines, you can almost expect that they have a tried-and-true process of finding great deals. But start talking to them even more and find out how they successfully source their deals. Is it from cold calling, emailing, door knocking, auctions, a foreclosure list, or some other way? I like knowing how my deal finders source their deals because it gives me a good idea of what works in that market, and when I connect with other deal finders, I get to compare the two strategies and make decisions for myself on which seems to work best.

Every single market and strategy I have pursued as an investor over the last decade started with me identifying an all-star deal finder who led me to the rest of my team. In addition to Kansas City, I have built teams in Ohio, Tennessee, Florida, and Arizona. I have also invested in over forty syndications, and the first person on my team was, you guessed it, an all-star deal finder. Even later, when I started in private lending, the first person on my team was the all-star deal finder. In this case, the deal finder happened to be me because once I became known for investing in real estate, many private lending opportunities came directly to me, so all I needed to do was use my own resources to build out the rest of my team.

Contractor

A common strategy for investors is to buy distressed properties that need renovations to either keep or flip (we will discuss this more in Chapter 9). This strategy is great, but it's impossible to do it passively if you do not have a rock star contractor on your team. The idea is that they are doing the work, not you.

The easiest way to find one is to ask your deal finder for a recommendation. However, once you get a name, you still need to do your own due diligence and vet the contractor.

You want a contractor who is licensed and bonded. Ask them for proof, and they should show it willingly. You also want to ensure that the contractor has extensive experience doing the type of project renovations that you need. You do not want to hire a contractor who has experience in flooring and cabinets but not in expanding the square footage of a property, especially if you want to add a room over the garage or a second floor to a ranch-style property.

Ask the contractor for photos of their previous work and a list of their clients you can talk to. Then ask the clients if they were satisfied with the work that the contractor did, if they came in on budget and on time, and whether there were any issues.

Once you hire the all-star contractor, establish a budget for the work that needs to be done and put it in writing. Make sure all the job details are in the contract and it is signed and dated by both of you. The contract should also state that any money spent above an agreed-upon amount should have to be a change order that you approve and sign off on.

The next part of the contract should have a timeline for every part of the renovation. Holding the contractor to a schedule and deducting payments when they miss deadlines is a great way to keep them on track (which should also be outlined in your contract). Time is money, so you do not want a situation where the contractor takes twice as long as they said to finish the job.

You should also include a payment schedule based on the completion of the contractor's work. I typically pay in four installments: an upfront payment, two payments in the middle of the work, and the last payment when the entire project is finished. I can't stress this enough: *Never* pay a contractor the whole renovation budget upfront. They can conceivably run away with the money.

Finally, if you are renovating an out-of-state property, ensure the contractor supplies you with regular photo updates. I also advise that you have someone else on your team pop into the property regularly (and perhaps unexpectedly) to make sure the work is being done.

> **NOTE:** If the idea of dealing with a contractor sounds too daunting for your first investment, I recommend doing what I did and buy a turnkey property. A turnkey property is already lease-ready and does not require a large renovation. The return you can earn in forced equity on a turnkey property decreases, but so does the risk of dealing with a contractor.

Property Manager

When you are a passive investor, the property manager is the most important person on your Core Four team next to the deal finder. This is a person or company who will be handling the day-to-day management of your investment property. You cannot be a successful passive investor without a rock star in this role.

The best way to find a qualified property manager is a recommendation from your deal finder. While I have said that a few times, it's important to note here that your deal finder might not be willing to share the names of their team members with you, so you may have to research them all on your own. You can also find trusted property managers that solve headaches and free your time with the BiggerPockets Property Management finder. You can learn more at www.BiggerPockets.com/bookpm.

The manager or management company should have experience in managing properties in your market and your asset class. For example, if you purchased a twenty-unit building, you want to hire a property manager who specializes in multifamily properties, not single-family properties.

Expect to pay your property manager somewhere between 8 and 10 percent of the gross rental amount every month. If the company charges more than 10 percent, that's a red flag. All my managers only charge 8 percent, and as I give them more units to manage, I will negotiate the percentage down further as they make more.

The best property managers are detail-oriented and organized. They provide updates when leases come to an end and consult with you when determining rental rates. For instance, if a tenant moves out after two years and they are paying $1,500 a month, the manager and I review the rental market breakdown and discuss an increase in the rent for the next tenant.

As you do with a contractor, once you find the property manager that you want to hire, you should both sign a management agreement contract that outlines how they will manage the property and what their fees are. For example, one of my managers keeps the first month's rent as their tenant placement fee when they place a new tenant, while another property manager in another market takes 75 percent of the first month's rent. All of this must be known upfront and agreed upon in writing.

You should also agree on when the manager will notify you about a building repair. For example, my managers take care of issues when they are under an agreed-upon cost (they still tell me about all repairs in the monthly reports). I like this system because I do not want to be called every time a plumber has to fix a clogged toilet, but I do want to be called if the AC needs to be replaced. So, you must know when and for what to receive a call/email.

Finally, every rock star property manager (or PM for short) should use software programs such as AppFolio to track where every dollar is going. It's a red flag to me if a PM would rather write in a ledger than use a software program. It doesn't mean that you hired a corrupt PM, but I would question why they are not using this modern-day technology.

Lender

The final member of your Core Four Team is your lender. Who you borrow money from is very specific to you, your financial situation, and your investment needs, such as the type of property you are buying. For example, if you are buying single-family homes, you may need to take out a different loan than if you are buying an office building.

What that means is your lending needs will differ if you are a W-2 earner compared to if you are a self-employed entrepreneur. A W-2 earner has an easier time qualifying for traditional loans, while a self-employed entrepreneur often has to jump through hoops to prove financial stability and creditworthiness. To find a lender start by asking your deal finder for referrals. You can also find lenders on your own by doing an online search in your area, asking other investors for referrals or talking to people on social media. BiggerPockets has a Lender Finder, which helps you find and compare lenders that have the best loans for real estate investors. Visit www.BiggerPockets.com/booklender to learn more. Start to build relationships with different lenders—big banks, local banks, national lending companies, private lenders, and so on.

Lenders will review loan options with you before you put an offer on a property. Otherwise, you can spend a ton of time analyzing a deal and then realize you don't qualify for the type of loan or amount of money you need.

Bonus Team Member: Accountant

Most likely, you already have an accountant who completes and files your taxes every year, but if you don't, you should get one before you start investing in real estate. An accountant is essential. They will help you open LLCs, advise you on tax savings and what expenses you can deduct, and so much more. I am by no means a tax or legal professional, so I recommend you discuss with your accountant about best tax strategies and business structures to consider before investing. But I will share with you how my team and I have set things up. I own individual LLCs for every single state I invest in. I also own a separate LLC for my lending business as well as my syndication investments because those businesses are different in nature from my properties. If I ever get into commercial real estate, I will likely have a separate LLC for that as well. Full transparency here, having multiple LLCs means you have to file taxes for each and begins to complicate your financial and tax picture, so I highly recommend you discuss your plans with a professional before making any of these decisions.

Not every accountant specializes in real estate investing, so make sure yours has the experience and knowledge you need. BiggerPockets also has a CPA finder, where you can search for top real estate finance experts to get a better tax strategy. Learn more at www.BiggerPockets. com/bookCPA.

Special Members

In addition to the Core Four, you may need other members on your team who are specific to your kind of investment.

Special Team Members for Private Lending

If you decide that private lending is the route you want to go, you will also need:

1. **Lawyer**: You are entering into legally binding contracts with borrowers and must have the right documentation and paperwork to protect yourself. I cringe when I hear about private lenders who use online boilerplate contracts as their lending documents. It's imperative that you have a lawyer who can write, or at least review, any loan document before you sign.

2. **Title Company**: If you become a private lender, it's important to have a title company that you like to work with that helps with the closing of your properties. The title company ensures that each transaction stays on schedule. They also facilitate the closing of the property for your borrower. I like working with the same title company as much as possible because they grow comfortable with my loan documents, and we have a seamless process in place that makes every closing great.

Special Team Members for Syndications

When investing in syndications as a limited partner, your *only* responsibility will be understanding the deal and the paperwork. The problem is that the paperwork can be extremely difficult to understand sometimes, and you may not know exactly what to look for when underwriting your deal. As a result, here are the additional team members you need on a syndication team:

1. **Lawyer**: You will be signing legally binding documents, so it's good to have legal counsel review them and notify you of any red flags.

2. **An Experienced Investor**: Early on in your passive investment journey, you may not know exactly how to review underwriting, what to look for, and whether a deal is a good one or not. Have the deal reviewed by a fellow experienced investor with experience investing in similar deals.

Special Team Members for Commercial Real Estate

1. **Lawyer:** Commercial real estate transactions are typically much larger and more complex. A lawyer is vital to reviewing the documents before you sign on the bottom line.

2. **Broker:** With commercial real estate, you are most often dealing with a broker who is your deal finder, but in my experience, the broker is also the person who is helping me find tenants. For instance, if I am buying an NNN lease (a triple net lease property—a commercial lease where the lessee pays rent, utilities, insurance, maintenance, taxes, and other expenses), the broker will find me the property and the small business to lease from me.

Trust, but Verify

When building out your team, you absolutely must trust, but verify. Do not just assume that every team member is doing what they are supposed to be doing. Double-check their work, ask questions, review statements, and so on, to be sure that you are holding them accountable to their job.

Each month that I passively worked for twenty total hours, at least five of them were spent verifying that the members of my team were executing. What did that look like? I made sure I received good investment opportunities from my deal finder. I reviewed progress reports from my contractors, and I confirmed that the work was done by getting progress pictures and property management statements. I also confirmed that every dollar was accounted for. I stayed in touch with my lender so I knew what interest rate I would receive on the next property and that they had all of the information they needed from me. This way, once it was time to close, we were ready.

Unfortunately, even with all your vetting and any glowing recommendations you get, sometimes a team member can become a problem. Your property manager or contractor may slack on the job and slowly let things creep in that they never did before, especially if they know you are not watching.

For this reason, I would schedule a last-minute trip to visit my properties during every off-season and meet with my team in every market I invested in. I did not want them to think that because I was a thousand miles away, I would never travel to check on them. By the way, I still do this today.

Once when I visited my Ohio property management team, I gave them only a week's notice about my arrival. When I got there, I found out exactly why one of the properties that had been vacant for three weeks still wasn't rented out. The management team was supposed to be painting the walls, fixing doors, etc. They said that they had, but when I went into the house, I could see that those things were not done. Before that, I had no issues with this property manager, but their business was growing, and they were hiring new employees and getting sloppy with their work for me.

I immediately requested a meeting with the owner of the property management company to discuss the issues and had them resolved immediately. If I did not verify that my property manager was doing the work for me, I am unsure how long they would have let that property remain vacant. This is just one example of why you must use a good portion of your time verifying every month.

Backups

Finally, you must expand your network by having a list of backups. It's great to find one all-star deal finder, contractor, property manager, and lender, but if you become too dependent on one team member and they start slacking, you are left scrambling. While I love my team, I have potential replacements right at my fingertips. This has served me well because if I ever think that something is not right or someone on my team is not giving me a good enough deal, I can also get a second opinion from someone else who is itching to replace them. If you do not have a replacement ready, you take more risks than you realize.

With my first property in Beech Grove, Indiana, I built a team all through one person who was, of course, a deal finder. This deal finder was working with new institutional buyers (larger corporations who wanted to buy up his inventory), and they were buying up his properties five to ten houses at a time. All of a sudden, he ghosted me. This was a problem because I had one property in Indiana but planned to buy several more. However, now my main contact had disappeared, and I did not have a backup deal finder to work with. This is why I ultimately decided to stop investing in Indiana. I learned a valuable lesson with that deal finder, so now I have a backup for every spot on every team of mine.

Building out a quality team while you're working a full-time job may seem overwhelming and time-consuming, but in reality, it's much easier than you probably realize. Having good teammates is essential, so don't get lazy with this step. In fact, this may be the single most important task you complete to build out your portfolio.

By now, I hope you see that this chapter and Chapter 6 easily fit together. Learning the language and the playbook seamlessly leads into finding your core team members. Then, having your team in place glides right into the standard operating procedures you will need in order to work together, which we will talk about next.

CHAPTER 8

STANDARD OPERATING PROCEDURES

> *"Systems run the business and people run the systems. Standard operating procedures are essential to creating a successful organization."*
>
> —Michael Gerber, author

I'm sure you're a busy person, and to do what you need to do every day, you probably already have some systems in place. For example, if you have children to get off to school on time every day, you know what time they need to wake up, eat breakfast, and get out the door. Lunches are made when you get up or before you go to bed and, if you are anything like me, you have your and your kids' clothes picked out the night before, all to make your morning a little easier.

When it comes to paying your bills, you probably already have systems in place to make sure they get paid on time. Maybe you write them in on your calendar or schedule them automatically, so they aren't missed. The passive real estate industry is no different. Investors like me thrive on creating systems, or what I like to call standard operating procedures (SOPs) that help me run my business more effectively and efficiently.

A standard operating procedure is an official term that companies and organizations use to carry out routine operations. These procedures are every step of what the staff or employees need to know to complete a task. When everyone follows the same SOP, there is less chance of mistakes or miscommunication, and it allows for a high level of efficiency.

It's hard for me to talk about SOPs without thinking about the history of McDonald's. If you didn't know, Ray Kroc was not the first founder of the franchise. Instead, the first McDonald's drive-in was opened in 1940 by two brothers: Maurice ("Mac") and Richard McDonald in San Bernardino, California. Eight years later, they changed their business so they could make food much quicker, serve more people, and eliminate the need for waiters and waitresses. They created SOPs, and it was a huge success.

A few years later, Ray Kroc, who was the distributor for a milkshake mixing machine, saw what the brothers were doing and was intrigued. He decided to become a franchise agent for them and ultimately launched McDonald's Systems in 1955. Kroc bought them out in 1961.

The McDonald brothers had created standard operating procedures so they could work quickly. Once Kroc had learned what those SOPs were, he was able to teach them and scale the business quickly. These were the linchpin to what has become today's fast-food industry.

SOPs are used across the board in business. I know we haven't covered the best real estate side hustle vehicles yet (trust me, it's coming), but that is intentional. When I first started investing in real estate, I had no idea what SOPs even were, so I had none in place. Because of this, I was winging every aspect of my side hustle and figuring it out as I went along. There is no reason to start your investing journey the same way I did. Instead, before we even get into the nitty-gritty of which side hustle vehicles you can invest in, I first introduce you to SOPs so you can start thinking about how important they are and how you need to incorporate them into everything you are doing with your investments.

As a passive real estate investor, you build teams and need things to run smoothly with each member. Creating and using SOPs with your deal finder, contractor, property manager, and lender will come in handy because the process from beginning to end will become replicable and consistent, which saves you time. Everyone will follow the same procedures and you will know exactly what to expect from each person you work with. It's important to introduce SOPs as soon as you develop a working relationship with any team member.

Like the McDonald brothers, I recommend that you create SOPs for every aspect of your passive real estate investment journey, right from the beginning. Here are a few SOPs you can create before you even buy a property:

- How you will communicate with your deal finder to find deals
- How often you will underwrite deals each week and which software or spreadsheet you will use to do so
- What your expectations with a contractor are and the processes you will use to hold them accountable
- Where/how you will store documents and stay organized

Again, I came nowhere close to doing this in the beginning, but if I could go back in time and do it all over again, these are things I would do right out of the gate. Once I finally decided to create SOPs, I felt as if I was working backward and it took longer than necessary to start incorporating them because I already had so much going on that I needed to rein in and gain control of. I learned this lesson so you don't have to. Set yourself up for success early.

Keep in mind that most of your team members (especially if they are truly all-stars) probably have their SOPs already in place, but they might not call them that. For example, a contractor might have a checklist of items they look at in a property to determine an estimated renovation budget. Ask them to walk you through every step of their process so you can understand how they do things. This question and their answers are what will give you a good sense of what their SOPs are. Make sure the process works for both of you, or ask them to make adjustments to meet your preference.

Review this before they start on anything.

As you continue in your journey, SOPs will become vital to scaling your investment portfolio. They truly are the beating heart of growing your business. Without them, you will find yourself having to be far more of an active investor than you can manage or intend.

I will now walk you through some of the main SOPs you should create to start and grow your passive real estate portfolio. Feel free to copy mine word for word, or just use them as a reference point to build your own.

Standard Operating Procedures for Your LLC

First, let's discuss why having a limited liability company (LLC) is a good idea. My number one reason is to limit personal liability. My LLC is the owner of my assets, so if someone wants to sue me, they go after the property and/or the other assets within the LLC, but nothing more. If the investment were in my name, everything I own could be in jeopardy.

The second reason I like having an LLC is the tax write-offs. By having an LLC, all the income and expenses are run through the LLC, which allows me certain tax benefits and write-offs that I normally wouldn't have access to. For example, I have to go look at properties often, therefore I am able to write off all/most of my travel expenses (flight, hotel, food, and gas).

It's important to note that an LLC is relatively inexpensive to open, which is yet another reason why I think it's a no-brainer to do.

Opening an LLC is one of many processes you should understand so you can do it effectively and efficiently. There is no limit as to how many you can open, so this is especially important if you're going to open more than one.

I open a new LLC for every single market I invest in. Once I invest in ten or more units in one market, I create an additional LLC. I do not want too many properties under one LLC. If a tenant were to ever try to sue me for something frivolous, they can go after only what is under that LLC. As a result, the more LLCs you have as you scale, the better.

However, you must strike a balance with this because each time you open an LLC, it costs money. In addition, there are more tax returns to do and operating agreements (documents that show who the owner of the LLC is) and bank accounts you have to keep track of with each one. I still recommend that you open an LLC in every state you invest in as well as an LLC for every separate business you have. I have an LLC for all my syndication investments and an LLC for my lending company.

I can't stress enough that you should set up the first LLC before you start investing. For me, opening one looks like this:

1. **Choose an LLC name**. Have trouble thinking of one? Use ChatGPT (chat.openai.com). I input what the core principles of my business are and some ideas that I have for the name and ask ChatGPT to give me five to ten suggestions. The system either gives me one that I use or at least sparks some ideas that I can go off of. For example, my own lending company's name is 42 Solutions. I knew I wanted a business name that had something to do with the number forty-two because that was my number for most of my high school, college, and professional football career. Make sure you run your LLC name by your accountant and lawyer so they can ensure there is no other local company with the same name.

2. **Contact your accountant.** My SOP is to use my accountant to set up my LLC, but your lawyer can open one too. I like using an accountant because they are less expensive and focused on how they can set up the LLC in a way to save on taxes. Lawyers are more costly and are focused more on the state and local laws. There is nothing wrong with that, but in the case of a real estate LLC, there are not many state or local laws to worry about, so I am better off saving money with my accountant. Whoever you choose, make sure both team members are aware of what you are doing. They will create the articles of organization for your LLC (in other words, all the documents you need) and submit them to the state's business administration office.

    You will receive an employer identification number (also called an EIN), which is similar to your Social Security number, but it's for business. Getting the EIN can take up to a week, so do not wait until right before closing on a property to start this process.

3. **Decide who gets what.** Once you have an EIN, your lawyer will draw up an operating agreement that outlines who owns how much of your LLC. This is where you need to decide how your business will be divided, if at all. Are you the sole owner? Will you have a partner? Will you have multiple partners? Do you want your wife/husband or kids to have equity in the ownership of the LLC?

Once you have the EIN documentation and your operating agreement, you can now open a bank account and credit card in this business name. Now you are ready to operate your business! Make sure you keep business and personal expenses completely separate from each other.

SOP for Evaluating a Market (Single-Family/Small Multifamily)

Once I find a location that I'm interested in, I follow my SOP for evaluating that market.

Consult with a Deal Finder and Property Manager

These team members have great insight and can help me identify where I should invest and the type of property I should buy in that area. For example, they will tell me what the best county is and which are the best cities and towns in that county. Then, digging even deeper they know which neighborhoods in those areas are the best to invest in (and contrarily which are the worst so I know what to say away from). In those neighborhoods, I will want to know about the school districts, etc.

Why do I care about the school district if I'm not sending my own children there? I want to buy a home in an area that is in demand because I know that tenants will want to live there.

Do Your Research

Remember, trust, but verify. Once my deal finder and PM give me their thoughts on an area, I do my own due diligence. My favorite site to use for this is www.bestplaces.net. This website is a one-stop shop where you can find information on the average price of homes, school ratings, crime ratings, job growth, population growth, average rental rate, and so much more. The paid version gives you a full market PDF, breaking all of this down in one document for you.

Create a Buy Box

If everything checks out, I create my buy box. This is a list of criteria that any property my deal finder sends me must meet. I use a combination of the return metrics (a quantifiable measure that can be used to estimate a property's performance) I want to reach and their market knowledge to help me decide on a good price range, neighborhood, and property type. I clarify that I do not want to see any deals that do not fit this buy box, because I don't want a ton of deals to review. The buy box may change over time, but it's a good starting place.

Here is my buy box right now for the Tampa market:
- Two to ten units
- Purchase price of $600,000–$1,200,000
- Value-add opportunity (not looking for stabilized assets)
- Class A or B location/neighborhood
- 7 percent cap rate or higher

That's it. If someone brings me a deal that doesn't fit within these parameters, I will not even look at it.

I have to point out that while I have my buy box, my deal finders have their own SOPs for finding deals. I let them procure the deals however they see fit, but I will ask them to only send properties to me that meet these criteria, and to clarify if the deal is an Urgent 1 or Urgent 2.

An Urgent 1 deal means if I want the property, I should evaluate it ASAP because it will likely become unavailable if I take too long. An Urgent 2 deal is for the properties that are most likely not going anywhere, and I have time to underwrite and make a decision.

I must note that all my deal finders do a good job of sending me some sort of initial underwriting on the deal. It isn't a deep dive—that is my responsibility—but they will give me an idea of what they think my CoC and NOI will be on the deal.

Use DealCheck

Once my deal finder sends me a deal, it's time to do my underwriting on the property and the market. Simply put, I will look at all aspects of a property and assess its value to determine if it's a good deal. To do this, I use a software program called DealCheck to underwrite all of my deals. I will input all the property's information and based on the facts I receive, I will determine whether or not I want to put in an offer. It's important to note that my role within the SOP for evaluating a deal is something I can do in an hour or less and can do it all from my phone. Using the internet and apps, I can quickly determine if a deal is worth putting in an offer on or not.

Put In an Offer

If the deal works for me, it's time to put in an offer. I need to decide if I should do it at the listing price or if I need to come in under the asking price.

If my offer is accepted and I go under contract to buy a property, I then enter the due diligence period of the transaction. This is the period when I will double-check my numbers and schedule both an inspection and an appraisal.

SOP for Renovating a Property

Renovating a property is a popular way to force equity (make a property more valuable). To do this as a side hustle takes having SOPs with your contractor, so the rehab does not take up more of your time than it should. If I am buying a property I know I will be renovating, I get my contractor involved and I will have an SOP with them as well. It looks like this.

Visit the Property

First, I schedule a time where my contractor can visit the property in person and do a room-by-room estimate of the work that needs to be done and the cost. They provide pictures of each room to give me a reference of what it looks like now and how they are recommending we change to it.

Provide a Scope of Work

After my contractor has visited the property, we talk about what renovations are needed and make sure we are on the same page. They then provide a detailed scope of the work and a breakdown of the proposed budget that we discussed.

Finalize Numbers

At this point, I should have received the inspection report that tells me all the things that may be wrong with the house and the appraisal confirming the current value of the house. I already have the potential scope of work that my contractor provided. Now I take all this information and ensure that the deal still makes sense to me. If it doesn't, then I cancel the transaction and get my deposit back. If it does still make sense, then I proceed with the purchase and make sure I am ready to put my plan into action upon closing.

Sign Contracts

Once I close on the property, my contractor and I sign a contract that lays out the exact agreed-upon budget as well as the timeline. This allows me to hold my contractor accountable for the project's timeline.

In this contract, I also like to include a draw schedule. This is when and how I pay the contractor. You never want to pay a contractor in full on the front end. Instead, I like to pay in three or four installments, depending on how big the project is. For example, I will pay 25 percent to start the project, and once the contractor has finished a portion, I will give them 25 percent more. I do not make the last payment until the entire job is done.

By putting this in the contract and not paying my contractor upfront, I can almost make sure they never run away with my money, and it keeps them motivated to get the job done. With this contract, you and the contractor know exactly what to expect from each other.

Before I make any draw payments to the contractor, I also have it in the SOP that they must send me updated photos of the work as it is being completed. Otherwise, they could tell me it's done to get payment when it's not.

I hope you can see that the amount of work I need to do as a passive investor when creating SOPs with my contractor is minimal. I let the contractor be the all-star they are, and I just need to review the numbers and oversee the progress of the renovation.

SOP for Managing Properties

When investing in real estate as a side hustle, you will likely be hiring a property management company to handle the day-to-day management of your property. Therefore, when creating SOPs for managing properties, you as the investor are concerned with managing the manager. The great thing is, most of the work is done upfront and you just need to review statements monthly. This is what it looks like for me.

Choose a Property Manager

I mentioned before that one of the best ways to find a property manager is by word of mouth. Your deal finder or contractor is the first place you should go for recommendations. After that, leverage Google and social media and/or ask around for the best property managers in the area where you are investing.

Learn Their SOPs

As I said earlier, it is unlikely that the property manager you go with will call their processes SOPs, but they certainly have them. I know this because they are running a business and, more specifically, a business that they have to scale to make profitable. This can't be done without having SOPs. It's your job as a passive investor to know what your property manager's SOPs are. The best way to do this is to start by reviewing the property management agreement that you will sign with them. This agreement gives great insight into how they do things. Make sure you understand it or ask questions if you don't. This is also the time to change anything you do not agree with.

Make sure you review their standard lease agreement with the tenants. This document helps you understand the rules they have set and the expectations they have of every tenant who will live in your unit. Finally, ask which software they use to manage properties and send payments as well as monthly and yearly statements to you, the owner.

Develop Your SOPs

Once you know what to expect from the property manager, it is time to decide what your SOPs will be. Here is an example of what I mean. If I learned that my PM sends out a monthly statement on the fifteenth of the following month, then I will create an SOP that around the twentieth of every month to review the statement I received. I will compare that with the money that hit my account to make sure they are the same. Then I will make sure there are no concerns about the statement that I need to ask about. For instance, if I see maintenance expenses increasing at one property for two straight months, I know that is something I want to dig into deeper.

Again, as the passive investor, all you need to do to manage your PM is have a plan to review the statements once a month when they are received. This is a process that can take an hour or less to do.

Standard Operating Procedures for Lenders

At this point, you probably have not bought a property yet. Hopefully your financial life is not all that chaotic, and I am catching you at the right time. Please take the time to create SOPs for documenting your personal and business finances. You will save so much time and headaches by doing so. One piece of advice I wish I had listened to early on in my investing journey was get your documents organized! When you apply for a loan, lenders ask for a lot of financial information, and if you are not already organized, you will be scrambling every time you have to go through the process.

Honestly, I wasn't very organized in the beginning, and as my portfolio grew, getting my documents together became harder and took much longer to do. I finally buckled down and spent about two weeks gathering all the documents and filing them digitally. There are sites like ShareFile, Google Drive, and Dropbox you can use to upload documents and save them with encryption. Organizing allowed easier access for me. You can choose to do this online or make copies and leave the documents in a file at your home. But in this day and age, I think online digital filing is the way to go. Below you will see that I have shared my lender package with you. I will let you review it so you can understand all the documents you will need to put in your digital file. Now, I will explain my process of gathering this information so that it's never too daunting.

Create Folders

Choose the filing platform you prefer and create a master lender folder. In that folder create four different folders: one for the current year and then the three previous years.

For every year you created, make an additional folder for every category I listed in my lender package, such as your personal and business tax returns, bank statements, and so on. The earlier you start this, the better. For me, it took ten hours of work, but those ten hours have saved me countless hours today.

Stay Updated

Once you have done the initial work of creating these folders and uploading the documents you need each year, you must make it a part of your SOPs to keep these documents updated. For instance, in March, ahead of the April 15 tax filing date, I upload every personal and business file created by my accountant in that year's folder in an effort to stay organized and prepared for filing season. Another example: In January of each year when all my bank account statements have been posted from December and I have the yearly statement, I spend an hour adding them to my folders.

Prequalified

As soon as I start putting offers in on homes, I reach out to my lender(s) to make sure they have the most updated documents they need. By storing all this information as I go, getting a prequalification letter from them is quick and easy. Before I even find a deal that I will close on, they have just about everything they need from me and I am prequalified to purchase the property.

Move Fast

By being prequalified and having all my documents in order, I can execute with speed when I find the right property to invest in. This is a major advantage for me!

Okay, I'll be honest with you. This work—while it doesn't take a ton of time—sucks. It's tedious, but it needs to be done and the more thorough you are, the easier the lending process will be. If you have the idea of getting organized this way, I recommend you hire a bookkeeper, executive assistant, and/or work very closely with your accountant. They can all play a role in helping you stay organized.

Paperwork Checklist

To get you started, this is a list of what is in my lender package, which I created under my company, 42 Solutions. It is everything that I document and how I do it. (I've also included it as a PDF download to keep with you or with your financial documents, which can find at www. BiggerPockets.com/sidehustlebonus.)

As I said, it's never too early to get these documents together, even if you're not close to buying a property. This way, though, once you are ready to apply for a loan, you're not wasting time. So what do you need to do?

- Upload a copy (front and back) of your driver's license.
- Obtain your most recent credit reports from all three major credit bureaus: Experian (www.experian.com); Equifax (www.equifax. com); and TransUnion (www.transunion.com). By law, you can get a free credit report once a year from each.
- Upload copies of the last three years of your state and federal tax returns, including all receipts, W-2s, 1099s, K-1s, etc., that you file with them.
- Upload your personal financial statement (PFS): This is a list of all your assets and liabilities. I recommend that you download a PFS template document online that you can fill out. In the chapter notes is an example of one I use and keep updated.
- Upload your personal bank statements: checking, savings, retirement, etc. I recommend uploading at least the past six months. These support your PFS.
- Upload a complete schedule of real estate holdings (once you start investing): This is a detailed breakdown of your real estate holdings, including purchase prices, loan amounts, down payment amounts, renovation budgets (if applicable), current rents, fair market values, comps to support those values, gross revenues, net operating incomes, mortgages, etc.
- Property Side: If you are requesting a loan in your LLC name instead of in your name, the lender will need to evaluate the deal and the entity information. Here are the documents you will need to have ready for them.
  - LLC Documents:
    - EIN
    - Articles of organization
    - Operating agreement

- Bank statements from all business accounts associated with your LLC.
- Property/Deal Details: If it is your responsibility to complete the underwriting and pro forma of the deal, you need to have the purchase price, rehab budget, fair market value (FMV) of property at purchase, and expected after repair value (ARV) once property is renovated.
  - **Comparative Market Analysis** (CMA): This shows all comps that support your underwriting.
  - **Appraisal:** When applicable, the appraisal is a formal evaluation of your property's value.

Someone once asked me if doing all this takes up too much of my time. I told them no; it actually does the complete opposite for me. It took a little time to gather everything together in the beginning, but then all I needed to do was update the documents regularly. Then, when I'm pressed up against a deadline to get a deal done and I'm busy, I already have everything the lender needs right in the file, ready to send to them. It allows me to be an extremely time-efficient passive investor!

Standard Operating Procedure for Filing Taxes

What I have found is that if you go through the process of building a thorough SOP for your lenders, most of that documentation is what your accountant needs to file your taxes. As I write this, I have five LLCs, so you can imagine how much paperwork I need to keep track of.

Open a Business Credit Card

I do not mix business and personal expenses on the same credit card. Early in my investing career, I made that mistake because I didn't make the extra effort to open business credit cards. I learned that being lazy on the front end made my life more difficult on the back end. How? Using the same credit card for both personal and business transactions meant that when it was time to file taxes, I had to sift through every transaction for the entire year and make note of which were business expenses. As a passive investor, I want to save myself time, so doing the upfront work of opening separate accounts is a no-brainer tip that I pass on to you.

Communicate with Your Accountant Year-Round

Tax planning is just as important as, if not more than, tax filing, so I like to keep my accountant in the know about any big decisions I make. For example, when I wanted to buy cars for my wife and me, I consulted with my accountant on the type I should buy and how much I could rationalize spending. My accountant told me that buying a car that weighs more than 6,000 pounds would allow me to write off the purchase, as long as I am using it for business. Well, my wife and I are both real estate professionals, and our cars are certainly used for business. So we were able to write those off. Checking in with my accountant helped tremendously with our car selection.

Other SOPs to Consider

- **Email:** One of the biggest time zappers is email. Think about how much time you spend checking emails, writing emails, and answering emails. An SOP that outlines when and how you track and respond to emails is a great way to guard your time and be effective with handling what's important to you.

- **Executive assistants:** At some point in your real estate journey, I believe that every passive investor should hire an assistant. Having someone help to manage your personal, work, and investing life is a game changer. Having an SOP with your assistant frees up your time because you can trust that they know exactly how you check and respond to emails, plan your meeting schedules, and the kind of hotels you like to stay at on vacation.

- **Social media scheduling:** Leveraging social media can become a huge advantage for you, but you are trying to give yourself more time not less, and social media is another time suck. Have a plan in place that outlines when you post—daily, a few times a week, or weekly. For me, I made a commitment to post every day for the entire year. I schedule my post in advance, anytime between 12:00 p.m. and 6:00 p.m., every day. Every two weeks I have a day that I record several videos in my office; I send these videos to my content manager who jazzes them up with cool captions and cover art and then sends them back so I can post.

- **Lawyer:** Having a clear SOP with your lawyer is very important. When I email my lawyer, there are some items I understand that may take him a week or two to review and respond to, but I like to make sure good communication is a part of my lawyer's SOP. If I email him, I am expecting a response of acknowledgment and a weekly update, even if that update is, "Hey, I still haven't gotten to this but I will soon." Another SOP my lawyer and I agreed to is that if I send him anything that is labeled "Urgent 1," it means I need it looked at ASAP. He will find time within twenty-four hours or pass the item to someone who can help me. I am careful not to abuse that, but sometimes things come up that simply cannot wait a week or two.

There's a saying from the Bible (Hebrews 12:11), "No discipline seems pleasant at the time, but painful. Later on, however, it produces a harvest of righteousness and peace for those who have been trained by it."

All of this seems like a lot of work (okay, I did say it sucks), but remember, you're saving yourself a lot of work later. I have seen many investors burn out because they did not create SOPs. They become stressed out because they work a nine-to-five (or longer if they are a doctor or firefighter or have kids to take care of after they work all day) and they are also trying to invest in real estate.

These SOPs are a *must*. Without the right team in place and the right SOPs, the path to becoming a passive investor can become way too overwhelming. There will be so much coming at you that you're not going to be able to handle it. As I've said, I didn't have a blueprint—you do. Follow it.

Right now, you are beginning to build a ridiculous amount of momentum. It might not feel like you're going anywhere, because you're still learning. You're getting organized. You're preparing. Just remember the man with the sharp axe from the last chapter. Preparation is everything, and now you know the next secret: SOPs are the secret sauce to passive investing success.

SECTION III CONCLUSION

If you follow the steps in this section, your axe will be sharpened, and you will undoubtedly be ready to start cutting down the tree. By now you know the language of real estate, the team members you may need (depending on the investment vehicle[s] you choose), and what to look out for as well as the standard operating procedures that will help you excel. As I built out my real estate side hustle, these were the missing pieces to my success. I did not know these things and paid the price many times along the way. But you don't have to. Expedite your passive investing journey by doing it right from the start.

Now it is finally the time to start talking about the actual passive investing vehicles that you can utilize as your side hustle.

SECTION IV
TAKE ACTION
INVEST THROUGH THE FOUR VEHICLES OF PASSIVE INVESTING

The only way to achieve your goals is to take the first step and never stop moving forward.

- Scale Up
- TAKE ACTION
- Prep for Action
- Increase Your Spread

*E*verything you've learned so far has prepared you for what you are about to learn in this section—this is all about *what* you can invest in.

This is the best part of take action because you *finally* learn about buying properties and getting into deals.

Throughout my real estate journey, I have studied, explored, and vetted just about every real estate investment strategy under the sun, often refining my thinking and strategy over and over. I could not have written this book when I had just five years of experience, because back then, I only had a thesis on what I *thought* was the path to success as a passive investor. I did not have a proven track record to back it. Now I do.

Everything I write about in this book I learned on the job, so to speak. Along the way, through a lot of trial and error, I identified what I consider to be the four best passive investing vehicles you can use to build your real estate side hustle. I call these investing strategies vehicles because they are the machines that you will drive to your destination.

What is that destination? It is where you have created enough financial stability that you get to do what you want when you want, where you want, and with whom you want. If you have a day job, you keep it because you *want* to, not because you *have* to. That's freedom.

One word of caution, though: Whatever you do, do not fall victim to shiny object syndrome. This is a real syndrome, and it means you are moving your attention to something new and shiny at the expense of whatever you are currently doing. For example, you want to be a passive real estate investor but find yourself chasing a real estate strategy, tactic, or advice that is trending in the industry yet goes against the mindset of a passive investor. Stay focused.

THE FOUR VEHICLES
The Ford F-150: Single-Family/Small Multifamily Investing

The F-150 is one of the most popular and affordable vehicles in America. It represents durability and versatility. Similarly, single-family and smaller multifamily properties have that same makeup. They are the most common way that real estate investors start and/or build their portfolios because the barrier to entry can be very low.

In 2024, in several cities across the country, you can still buy a three-bedroom, two-bathroom single-family home in a good neighborhood for less than $200,000. This lower entry point and ability to use debt is a comfortable feature for many investors. Pretty much everyone understands the use of a single-family home, making investors feel comfortable buying one as an investment. These properties can become fix-and-flips, short-term rentals, or long-term rentals, making them versatile investments. Additionally, they have proven to be durable as an investment by thriving in many different market cycles across the country, and that's another reason I have them pegged as the Ford F-150 of passive real estate investing.

The Range Rover: Syndications

With a higher ticket price than the F-150, the Range Rover represents a vehicle of luxury and class. Similarly, syndications have the same profile in real estate investing because they are suited primarily for what's called accredited investors.

Syndications provide multiple investors with an opportunity to pool their money to buy large properties that they would otherwise not be able to—or wouldn't want to—purchase on their own. To me, it is cool to say you invested in a large 200-unit apartment complex or office space the same way it is cool to pull up to dinner for date night in a Range Rover.

The Audi Q7: Private Lending

The Audi Q7 represents affordable luxury. It has the technology, design, and comfort but for a fraction of the cost of high-end luxury vehicles like the Range Rover or the Rolls-Royce Cullinan (our next vehicles). Similarly, you need access to capital to be a private lender, but it does not have as high of a threshold to get in as syndications or commercial real estate. You can utilize your retirement accounts or the equity in your personal or investment properties to lend to other real estate professionals. You can lend whatever amount you are comfortable with. When executed well, private lending can be a great passive income generator. You get some of the same benefits as syndications or commercial real estate (especially cash flow) but for much less capital. How much capital exactly is up to you and the borrowers you can find who want your money.

When executed well, private lending can be a great passive income generator.

Rolls-Royce Cullinan: Commercial Investing

The Rolls-Royce Cullinan may be the most luxurious car on the market, and its lofty price tag reflects that. For this reason, the barrier to owning a Cullinan is extremely high. Those who drive one are making a statement—they are declaring that they are among the wealthy and are sophisticated, successful, have high-end taste, and likely make serious money.

Similarly, commercial real estate typically has the highest barrier to entry, cost-wise. It is typically reserved for people and companies who can navigate the landscape of commercial loans, property management, software, raising capital, and so much more. There is risk involved, and it's very similar to running a business. Truth be told, if you can successfully own and manage commercial properties passively, you have likely become an expert in building teams and SOPs because you will see that this vehicle has more nuances than the others.

In the next four chapters, we will get into the nitty-gritty of each vehicle and how to best get into them as a passive investor.

Now, let's drive to success!

CHAPTER 9

FORD F-150
Single-Family/Small Multifamily Investing

"Ninety percent of ALL millionaires become so through owning real estate."

—Andrew Carnegie, industrialist and philanthropist

To start, I will be referring to *all* properties up to four units as single-family homes for the rest of this book. Banks and mortgage companies treat financing for multifamily properties up to four units the same way they treat financing for a single-family home. The standard thirty-year fixed mortgage that is used to buy a single-family home can also be used to buy a duplex, triplex, or fourplex.

The Ford F-150 truck is one of the most common vehicles on the road. Wherever you live in America, I highly doubt that you can drive for ten minutes without passing at least one. Similarly, single-family properties are the most common real estate investing vehicle, so I call them the F-150.

Before investing in your first single-family property, there are three things you need to consider:

1. **Funding**: Funding will dictate how you approach the next two items—location and strategy. How much of your capital do you have to invest? What lending sources do you have access to? Do you plan to use OPM? Do you plan to use creative financing?

When you look at all funding options, how much money do you have to invest?

2. **Location**: Once you determine how much you have to invest, you can look at where you want to invest. Do you want to buy a property where you live, or will you consider investing in one that's out of state? If you are like me and live in a fairly expensive real estate market, you may choose to invest elsewhere. Where to invest is a very personal choice, but back it up with logic. Why are you choosing the area you are to invest?

3. **Strategy**: This is where it gets tricky for many investors—deciding which single-family strategy makes sense for you (turnkey, BRRRR, fix-and-flip, long-, mid- or short-term rentals, etc.). Many investors get stuck in the cycle of hopping from one strategy to the next, trying to get a grip on what they should do. An example of this is a passive investor who commits to the long-term rental strategy but, after two houses, falls victim to shiny object syndrome and jumps into Airbnb investing because he has a buddy making a killing with that. Then he meets a contractor who tells him about fix-and-flips, so that becomes his next deal, and so on.

Funding

Before I started buying properties in Cleveland and Kansas City, I had increased my spread so much that I had a nice lump sum of money ready to invest. I was highly motivated to get my passive income to reach my TMI number as quickly as possible, so I bought the properties in cash. This way, whatever I received in monthly rent from my property manager was pocketed as cash because I had no mortgages to pay. Every dollar contributed to reaching my TMI number.

On average, I spent about $100,000 per house. Each property was rented for between $1,000 and $1,300 per month. Before I purchased them, I ran the numbers and calculated how many properties I would need to buy and the cash flow they would need to bring, net of all the expenses. That would be how many I would need to buy over a three-year period. By buying these properties in cash and keeping my fixed and variable expenses low, I reached my TMI number very quickly!

I completely understand that you might not want to or be able to afford to buy multiple single-family properties in cash. I chose to buy in cash because I had enough capital to do so and, as a result, the amount of cash flow I brought in every month increased. I think it's important for me to remind you of the work you did in section one (or will do) to increase your spread. Because of that you will have more capital to invest, but I must point out here that using debt is a great option in most cases because it allows your dollar to go further.

What I mean by that is with the same amount of cash I bought those single-family properties, I could have used leverage and only put 25 percent down and bought four times the amount of properties that I did. This is not the direction I started with but a perfectly good option with probably much more upside.

Using debt allows you to grow your net worth faster because you can buy more properties, and the rent from the tenants will pay down the loans over time. Using cash, you may only be able to buy one property at a time, if that.

Now you may be asking me if using debt is generally better, then why didn't I do that. Yes, buying more properties would increase my net worth faster, but it meant that each property would cash flow less because I would have a mortgage to pay on the properties. That is why for my first few properties, I chose cash flow over growth. After a few years of owning these properties, I ended up refinancing and getting most of my capital out to buy more assets.

You will need to decide whether you will put a premium on cash flow or growth. There is no right or wrong answer. It is based on your spread, capital, financial position, and what is most important to you at that time.

If you decide to use debt, what kind of loan will you need? In Chapter 2, I reviewed your options: traditional loans, hard money/private loans, DSCR loans, or portfolio loans. I also reviewed raising capital as an option. How you fund your first purchase is very personal because it will depend on your financial position (income and credit score, for example), risk tolerance, and strategy.

Risk tolerance is how much risk you are willing to endure with your investment, and it plays a major role in your choice of financing. For instance, if you are someone who doesn't like a lot of risk, then taking out a traditional loan might be the right option for you. Traditional loans are historically less risky because they have the lowest interest rates and the longest terms; the low interest rate allows you to have a manageable payment while the long term locks in that mortgage amount for thirty years. If you are someone willing to take on more risk, hard/private money loans are the opposite; typically, they have the highest interest rates and the shortest terms, so with high interest and short term you have the pressure of a high monthly payment *and* you will have to pay back the loan in a short time. This adds a ton of risk, but it makes sense in certain investment strategies, like fix-and-flips. The next question to ask yourself is how much debt are you willing to put down on the property? The higher the LTV, the higher the payment and the higher your inherent risk is. I have a conservative nature, so I would rather have a smaller portfolio of properties with a lower LTV than a higher LTV and way more properties. I sleep better at night knowing my debt is low, but others may say I am crazy, and I should be using leverage to buy as much as I can.

This all boils down to your risk tolerance and overall financial strategies.

 **SIDELINES**

UNDERWRITING

One of the most important things about investing in single-family properties is your ability to underwrite deals. Basically, this means running the numbers to ensure that the deal is right for you. To be honest, this was a major hurdle for me early on in my investing journey. I had no idea how to underwrite a deal and how to gather the information I needed to do this accurately. Here's an example of what I mean: To properly underwrite the deal, you need to get an accurate assessment of what property taxes will be, what the insurance will be, what the expected rental rate will be, and many other things. I did not know how to gather this kind of information or how to tell whether it was correct. But worse is the fact that I did not have the expertise in using Excel to create my own formulas to find the metrics I mentioned above.

What frustrated me the most was that I would meet active investors with fancy Excel calculators that broke deals down for them. And here I was, a passive investor wannabe who had to send the deal to other investors for them to run the numbers for me. If I am being real, it was inefficient, and I was embarrassed.

But my life changed when I came across DealCheck, an app that pulls data directly from Zillow and runs full reports on a property in minutes, providing a detailed breakdown of everything you need to know about the property and the investment opportunity. One thing I must note is that it pulls data from Zillow, which is known not to be 100 percent accurate. So while it's a great initial marker, you should confirm the data it pulls from Zillow before you move forward with a purchase. Unless you have a day job in finance or have some kind of background working with spreadsheets and don't mind building out your own, I highly recommend downloading DealCheck. It is a must-have. I have been in the passenger seat, on my way to watch my daughter play soccer, plugging in a property address to get a general idea of what my return will be.

Do you remember the metrics and equations we went over in Chapter 6—CoC, ROI, IRR, cap rate, and so on? DealCheck runs them all for you. You can change specific metrics to match your situation, but that's easy.

For example, plug in the address of the property you want to buy, and DealCheck pulls reports as if you were buying the property with a loan at 5 percent. However, let's say that you know your lender will be charging you 6.5 percent, and you plan to put 30 percent down. You can easily change those numbers within DealCheck, and it will recalculate the entire deal for you in seconds.

My favorite DealCheck feature (it comes with the higher monthly paid service) is the ability to print branded PDF reports with your personal or business logos.

I can plug numbers in on a potential deal, calculate my offer, print it out, and have my business and deal information as if it was a document I created in Excel myself.

Another cool feature is that DealCheck works directly with RentCast (www.rentcast.io/), another software program that views rent prices and comps for any property in the United States. It predicts long-term rents for whatever property you choose, and it pulls comps of other properties for rentals and sales. This software literally does 90 percent of the work for you. All you need to do is refine or double-check the numbers.

For instance, I know that my property will go through a mid-level re-hab (cosmetic fixes like paint, flooring, and cabinets), and I think I can charge $2,500 for rent instead of the current $2,100 once it's done. Deal-Check doesn't know about the rehab, so their recommended monthly rent may be listed as $2,100. I will need to change that. When I do, it updates all the reports and returns metrics to reflect the numbers I put in. If you cannot tell, DealCheck has been a game-changer for me when it comes to evaluating single-family properties!

Location

Passive real estate investors are making money in every city and state across the country because you truly can invest from anywhere. If you live in New York, you can invest in a property in Oregon. If you live in Texas, you can invest in a property in Montana, and so on. Wherever you choose to invest, find a market that you will commit to. It is a waste of your valuable time as a passive investor to choose a market, find funding, build a team, and develop SOPs to buy only one property in that market. It is much more effective to identify a market where you can commit to buying several deals. But how do you identify the right market for you?

First, start by researching properties where you live or have lived before. Don't worry—I am not suggesting you need to spend forty hours this month doing market research on every city you ever lived in. Simply use Google to find metrics that matter to you, such as the average home price, population growth, job growth, etc. You are looking for positive signs showing that the market makes sense for you to invest in. For your first purchase, investing in markets you are familiar with is probably your best bet. If these markets do not work for you, keep looking.

When I first started researching where I should invest, the markets I had connections to were Phoenix, Los Angeles, and New York City. I did a quick Google search on the average single-family home prices in each market (Phoenix, Arizona, was $250,000 at the time; Los Angeles, California, was $430,000; and New York, New York, was $499,000). All these prices (yes, even Arizona) seemed too high for me then, so I crossed them off my list and started looking elsewhere. I have a low risk tolerance, especially back in 2014, so buying a property for $250,000 in Phoenix intimidated me. Keep in mind that just because I decide that a market is too pricey for me, or someone tells you that a market is too pricey for them, does not mean that it is too pricey for you.

In hindsight, if I had taken that leap and invested in an Arizona property back then, I would be a happy man today because the market grew substantially, and I would have more than doubled my money. At the time, though, it did not fit my risk tolerance, and that was something I was willing to accept.

To find the right market for me, I kept researching and asked around about other markets. At a real estate meet-up in Arizona, my partner at the time and I met an investor who was buying properties in Indiana. He told us about the market and the team he had in place there. I learned that Indiana had turnkey properties that were really nice and fully renovated for less than $100,000 each and were bringing in close to $1,000 or more in rent. I could buy fully renovated properties in good neighborhoods in Indiana for less than $100,000? Sign me up!

The story behind how I started investing in Tampa, Florida, is very similar to this. I was a guest on Kathy Fettke's podcast *The Real Wealth Show,* and she and I hit it off. We kept in touch, and I learned more about her and her husband Rich's company, *RealWealth,* where they connect investors with vetted turnkey providers across the country. I told her I was interested in investing in a new market and asked her what city she would recommend. She recommended Tampa. She then connected me with her Tampa turnkey provider at the time, David Shaw.

Just like that, I met my deal finder, David, and started learning about the market reviewing some of David's current and former deals, and looking at the appreciation growth in certain areas of Tampa. All this data supported the fact that this was an incredible market to invest in. In the offseason of 2021, I went to Tampa to visit and meet David and his team (contractor and property manager). I felt so confident with them and the market that I decided this was the perfect location for my first value-add investment (a property I planned to renovate in order to add value to it). David helped me purchase a duplex and a six-unit property in Tampa, and I hired his contractor to renovate the properties and his property manager to get them rented out.

> **TIP:** Follow Dave Meyer on BiggerPockets (www.BiggerPockets.com/users/davem27) and Instagram (@datadeli) to learn about some of the best markets to invest in today. He is fantastic at identifying markets with great paths of growth!

However, one thing I did not consider when I invested in Indiana and Ohio but I do now is the value of investing in a city that I do not mind visiting. As a passive investor, you don't have to visit your out-of-state properties, but I would recommend that you do. Once a year, I visit every market where I own properties, even if it's just for a day. In doing so, you can check that your properties are being properly managed and maintained. You can connect with the team you put in place, so they know that you are on top of things and have expectations. And, while you are there, you can look for more properties.

I bought properties in Cleveland, Ohio and visited them once a year, right after the football season ended in January or February. Man, it was cold! On top of that, there was never anything I wanted to do in the area, and I dreaded the trip every time. Contrarily, I own properties in Kansas City, which is still cold, but it's a fun city, and they have some of the best barbecue I have ever eaten. Plus, my wife has family there, so it always makes that trip worthwhile. Visiting my Tampa properties is also amazing. There are great restaurants and beaches there—the vibes I love the most! When I first started investing, I did not care what city I invested in as long as I was going to make money, but now I see the value in owning in cities you enjoy visiting.

Some other important factors to consider when deciding which market to invest in are:

- **Appreciation rate:** How much are the values of homes going up in that particular market? For instance, Kansas City is known for being a slower annual appreciation market, growing at 4.19

percent since 2000, while Arizona is historically known as a fast-appreciating market, growing at 5.29 percent since 2000 (both according to www.neighborgoodscout.com).

- **Job growth:** Is the job growth in your city of choice above or below the national average? It's a great sign to see healthy job growth wherever you want to invest. That means people will need a place to live.

- **Rental rate:** Are rents in your market going up or down? If rents are going up, that means there is high demand and low inventory in the area, and you can get top dollar to rent your property out.

- **Crime rate:** Is the crime rate in your market above or below the national average? The first thing I look at when researching a property is the crime rate. If it is 3 percent or higher than the national average, I want nothing to do with that city. I do not want to own properties in neighborhoods I would not feel comfortable driving through at night! If it's at or below the national average, I take that as a sign that it's a safe area to invest in.

- **Population growth:** Is the population increasing or decreasing in your market? If more people are leaving the city or town you want to invest in than are coming in, it should be cause for concern. Population growth that trends down typically means that rental rates will probably decrease in the future as well.

All these factors impact one another. If job growth decreases, then population growth will most likely decrease too because people needing a job will leave the area. If residents leave town, that will impact the demand for places to live, which directly affects rental rate. This is why understanding these factors can be so important in deciding a market to invest in. Remember, in the last chapter I recommended BestPlaces. net to use to review this type of information.

Strategies

It's smart to start your passive real estate journey with a strategy. If you fail to plan, then you have planned to fail. The worst thing an investor can do is buy a property without having a clear plan for what they plan to do with it. Instead, understand the local market, what type of property works in that area, and what is best for your own goals.

Use the information from identifying your funding and location to then decide what type of property you want to invest in. Then decide what you are going to do with that property. For example, will you buy a turnkey beachfront property and then rent it out long-term to one tenant or use it as an Airbnb short-term rental to multiple tenants? Will you rehab a distressed four-unit property that you bought near a hospital for a discount and use it as a short-term rental to medical students or traveling nurses?

There is no right or wrong answer on the type of property you should invest in and how to use it. What is important is that you understand the difference between each type and then decide what fits the criteria you are looking for.

There are two categories of single-family properties you can buy:

- **Stabilized properties:** These are properties that need little to no work. There are three types:
  - **New builds:** I classify a property as a new build if it's been built within the past three years and is still in pristine condition. These properties often come with builder warranties on big-ticket items such as the roof.
  - **Turnkey:** These properties may or may not be new but are in good livable condition (the term comes from being able to just "turn the key" and move in). They either already have a tenant in place or are ready to go and could immediately place a tenant after you purchase it.
  - **Light rehab:** These properties need very little work to be rentable. Light rehabs include alterations like changing out the backsplash, faucets, hardware, and/or appliances. When I purchased light rehabs in the past, I painted the inside/outside of the house and updated the bathroom, and the property was ready for the tenant to move in.

A big drawback about buying stabilized single-family properties and placing a long-term tenant is that the amount of profit you can make on these deals annually is not going to change or impact your life much.

For example, you buy a three-bedroom, two-bathroom property for $160,000 in Kansas City. After all expenses are paid—including mortgage, property management, repairs and maintenance, and putting money toward the CapEx budget—you are expecting to net $200 a month on this property. Two hundred dollars a month might not seem like a lot. In fact, it would send many investors running somewhere else. After all, that is only $2,400 a year profit and can be wiped out with just one major issue on the property. True, but consider the long-term picture. That $200 cash flow today can turn to $500, $600, or even $1,000 a month five to ten years from now. Meanwhile, the property will most likely appreciate from $160,000 to $240,000 or more in that same period of time.

Now consider all the tax benefits of owning this same piece of real estate, like depreciation, the ability to complete a 1031 exchange, and the ability to write off operating expenses, taxes, and insurance payments.

Finally, do not forget that your tenants are paying down the mortgage over these years, which is increasing your equity, one payment at a time. So that property that netted you $200 could still be a worthy investment. It may not excite you enough in the short term, but remember you're in this for the long haul, and that property can be impactful years from now.

⭐ SIDELINES

As soon as you start to build a single-family portfolio, it is imperative that you start to put money aside for CapEx. In the example above, the single-family property would only generate $2,400 of profit each year, so if the HVAC needed to be replaced it could very well wipe out the whole year's earnings and likely more.

The best way to have money to cover repairs is to allocate a portion of the rent money for future CapEx or repairs. I like to put 5 percent aside each month. I also have a CapEx account that I fund until it reaches at least $10,000 per property I own.

I've been told that it's a bit excessive and I could reduce that amount, but I am sleeping very well at night knowing that just about anything can happen with any of my properties, and I have capital put aside to pay for it. I keep it in a money market account where, as of 2024, I am earning about a 4.5 percent return annually.

I compare my CapEx account to an emergency fund in my personal life—hopefully you never have to use it, but you will be glad you have it if/when you do! If you do not fund a CapEx account and your property either is vacant for longer than you expected, or a major expense comes up, you could find yourself in a challenging spot where you can't fix the property or are forced to sell it for a loss.

Funding this account is a priority because it gives me the certainty that I can withstand any issue with my properties.

Funding a CapEx account should be easier now because you have increased your spread and you are still working, so the excess income can fund this account.

Your goal as an investor is to generate income for financial freedom. Long-term rentals align well with this, thanks to their stability.

Still not sold? I get it. What, then, is the solution to increasing that monthly cash flow? Here are a few options:

- **Cash is king:** If you want a higher monthly income from real estate, one option would be to put more cash down when you buy a property, assuming you have it, of course. Buying properties fully in cash was a strategy I chose when I started my real estate journey. A property may only bring in $200 net expenses, but buying that same property in cash could bring in over $1,000 a month. It's because I do not have a mortgage to pay, so any rent money goes directly to me. That's what I was looking for.

  If after all operating expenses, you are earning $1,000 a month from a property that you bought in cash, you get that full $1,000 every month. If you have a $500 a month mortgage payment, then you make that payment first and are only bringing in $500 a month. So how much you put down as the down payment as well as the interest rate you get will impact the net amount you get to pocket every month.

- **Scale:** If you do not have more cash to put down or the desire to put cash down, scaling will become important for you if you want to make more passive income. Remember, buying one property for a $200 monthly cash flow might not make much difference to you in the short term, but buying ten starts to change the narrative for the long term. Develop a game plan to buy several properties over a few years. Your monthly cash flow will increase, and it will put you in a position to grow a large net worth because you own more assets that are all appreciating.

- **Strategize:** Consider other passive real estate strategies, such as mid-term, short-term, or fix-and-flipping. These strategies generate more cash flow than a traditional long-term rental.

- **Drive a different vehicle:** If you are hung up on generating a higher cash-on-cash return, consider private lending where you can generate 10 to 15 percent on your money annually.

4. **Distressed properties:** Because of age or long-term neglect, these properties are in poor condition and need renovation. There are two different rehab levels for distressed properties:

   - **Mid-level rehab:** This rehab is just a really good facelift. You will likely need to replace flooring, cabinets, bathrooms, fixtures, paint, and so on. Depending on the contracting team, a mid-level rehab can take anywhere from a few weeks to a few months to be completed.

- **Full rehab**: A property that needs a full rehab is in very bad condition and possibly even unlivable. You will likely have to do everything listed for a mid-level rehab, as well as replace plumbing, electrical, roof, and windows. Depending on the property, you might possibly change the floor plans or even add square footage. Full rehabs can sometimes take up to a year to complete before you can sign a tenant.

Pros and Cons of Stabilized vs. Distressed as a Passive Investor:

STABILIZED PROPERTIES

Pros:	Cons:
Will cash flow within the first month or two	You will most likely pay market price or close to it
Do not need to deal with or rely on a contractor (even on a light rehab, usually your property manager can handle)	Due to paying market price, your return potential is not as high as distressed properties
Getting a loan is relatively easier and charges the lowest interest rates	Unless it's a brand-new property, you must factor in CapEx and money for repairs still

DISTRESSED PROPERTIES

Pros:	Cons:
Because they are in such bad shape, you can typically buy these properties for a steep discount, giving you instant equity	Must rely on a contractor to handle the rehab on time and on budget
Can increase value and force more equity through rehab	Will not be profitable until rehab is completed, and you can rent it out
Can decrease future CapEx and repairs by addressing most issues during the rehab	Getting a loan is more difficult and usually has a higher interest rate

Single-Family Investing Strategies
Strategy 1: House Hacking

This strategy is for passive investors who will buy a single-family home and live in it while renting out parts of it to someone else. House hacking helps you offset your own primary living expenses. It's a great way to dip your toes into investing and managing tenants. However, from my experience, house hacking works best for younger and/or single passive investors who do not mind making some lifestyle sacrifices. If you house hack, you will most likely deal with other people in your personal space, so make sure you are comfortable with that.

If I had not made it into the NFL, my plan was to get a good job and then invest in a duplex. I would have lived in one unit and rented out the other. Considering your financial goals and lifestyle preferences, house hacking can be a smart strategy to kickstart your real estate investment journey.

PROS OF HOUSE HACKING

- **Income generation:** By renting out an extra bedroom in your own house or the other units in your duplex, triplex, or fourplex property that you also live in, you can generate rental income.
- **Lower living expenses:** House hacking allows you to live in a property with reduced or no mortgage payments because the rent from other tenants will cover it, making it a cost-effective housing solution. Remember, housing is most people's biggest fixed expense and house hacking reduces or eliminates that expense.
- **Building equity:** While you are paying down the mortgage with the rental income, you're also building equity in the property. This will become a valuable asset time.
- **Real estate investment exposure:** House hacking provides an entry point into passive real estate investing with a manageable level of risk, especially if you buy a property that you can afford on your own. Your tenants' payments are a plus, not a necessity.
- **Tax advantages:** You get all the tax benefits of owning real estate, including deductions for mortgage interest, property taxes, and operating expenses.

CONS OF HOUSE HACKING

- **Sacrificing privacy:** Living in a single-family or multifamily property with your tenants means sharing common spaces with them.
- **Property management responsibilities:** House hacking is the only time I would say it makes sense for a passive investor to also be the property manager. It does not make sense to hire another property manager when you are living inside your own house or perhaps in the next unit. With that said, you will be the one who has to collect rent every month and handle any complaints or

repairs. While this is still passive because it does not take much time to knock on the door of your own house to collect rent, it could definitely be inconvenient.

- **Tenant turnover:** The people you find as tenants will determine the stability of your rental, but there is still a chance you will deal with tenant turnover. If you are renting out a room, some tenants just want to do so temporarily, but if they are renting a full unit from you, they will probably sign a longer lease and your turnover rate will be lower.
- **Limited property choices:** Not all properties are suitable for house hacking, so finding the right one that meets your needs can be challenging. For example, if you want to rent out more than just a room, you need to find a single-family property that comes with a guest house or a basement where a tenant can have their own private space. Otherwise, you will be sharing common areas.

Strategy 2: Long-Term Rental

The long-term rental strategy is when you sign a tenant to a lease that is one year or longer.

If this is the strategy you want, you are more or less trying to set it and forget it. Most of my properties have long-term tenants who, hopefully, stay for at least two to three years. The longer they stay, the better it is for you. When a tenant leaves, you have to deal with turnover costs and/or a vacancy period while your property manager is trying to find a new tenant. This can hurt your overall ROI.

Investing in long-term rentals means choosing quality tenants. Remember when we talked about hiring a property manager and knowing how they work? In this case, it's important to know how they choose tenants. In some cases, property managers put a premium on placing tenants fast. As a result, they do not have a good vetting process and can unknowingly lease your property to problem tenants. The last thing you want is to get stuck with a tenant who causes problems, doesn't pay on time, or destroys your property. I tell my managers that I would rather they take a few weeks to find a quality tenant for me as opposed to quickly leasing to a tenant who is going to cause problems.

I know an investor whose tenant of three years had moved out and left behind a disaster. Dog and cat poop were all over the place. There were holes in the wall. The doors were broken. The house smelled like smoke, and so on. Of course, in this case the investor kept the security deposit, which helped to cover some of the expenses of cleaning and repairing the unit. However, this unit was in such bad shape that the investor had to pay out of his pocket to get the property back to a rentable state. In my opinion, with good property management, issues like this can be mitigated.

I also make sure that my property managers go inside the units periodically. If the property manager had inspected that unit from time to time, they would have seen that it was not being taken care of and could have addressed the issues before they got out of control. As a passive investor, if you are choosing long-term rentals as your strategy, you need to work with and depend on your property manager so that the overall experience and expectations are as positive as possible.

PROS OF LONG-TERM RENTAL

- **Stable income:** Long-term rentals provide a steady and predictable rental income stream, offering you financial stability.
- **Reduced vacancy rates:** Compared to short-term rentals, long-term rentals typically experience lower vacancy rates, minimizing income gaps between tenants.
- **Lower turnover costs:** With tenants staying for extended periods of time, you'll likely incur fewer turnover costs, such as cleaning, repairs, and marketing to find new tenants.
- **Lower utility costs:** It's widely expected that in a long-term rental, the tenant will pay their own utility costs, reducing the financial burden on the property owner.
- **Property wear and tear:** My long-term tenants tend to take care of my properties better than short- or mid-term tenants do.

CONS OF LONG-TERM RENTAL

- **Reduced rental income potential:** Stable, long-term rentals may offer lower rental rates compared to short-term rentals, potentially limiting your overall income.
- **Limited flexibility:** Long-term leases will restrict your flexibility to increase rental rates quickly.
- **Market sensitivity:** The success of long-term rentals is influenced by the local real estate market, economic conditions, and the demand for rental properties.
- **Eviction challenges:** If issues arise with long-term tenants, the eviction process can be time-consuming, and navigating legal procedures can be complex.

Strategy 3: Mid-term Rentals

The mid-term rental strategy involves leasing a property for a period that is typically between one and six months. It is a strategy that is picking up steam across the country, especially if you happen to buy a property in a state where people like to visit at certain times of the year. For example, Arizona attracts a lot of snowbirds from the cold states during the winter. They leave their cold state from November to February and turn in their winter coats for golf clubs in the desert.

Another successful mid-term rental is buying a property near a major hospital. These hospitals attract travel nurses who come to work for three to six months at a time, and a mid-term rental is exactly what they are looking for.

PROS OF MID-TERM RENTALS

- **Increased income stability:** Mid-term rentals often provide a more stable income than short-term rentals. Having tenants for a longer time reduces the risk of frequent turnover and vacancies.
- **Higher rental rates:** Mid-term rentals usually generate higher rents compared to traditional long-term leases. Tenants often pay a premium for the flexibility and furnished units.
- **Reduced management overhead:** While not as hands-off as long-term rentals, mid-term rentals usually require less management compared to the constant turnover of short-term rentals. It strikes a balance between income and operational ease.
- **Local market demand:** Assessing the local market demand for mid-term rentals is crucial. Cities with a transient workforce, tourists, or students often present suitable conditions for this strategy.

While mid-term rentals offer quite a few advantages, you need to be aware of the potential drawbacks.

CONS OF MID-TERM RENTALS

- **Potential vacancies:** While less frequent than short-term rentals, mid-term rentals can still face periods of vacancy, especially during off-seasons or economic downturns. A great example of this is in Arizona. You will have a much tougher time placing a mid-term rental in the summer when it's 110 degrees or hotter every day (all the snowbirds are gone).
- **Limited tenant pool:** The market for mid-term rentals may be smaller compared to traditional long-term leases. This could limit

your potential tenant pool, making it crucial to understand your local market demand.

- **Furnishing costs:** Offering furnished rentals is a common practice in mid-term strategies, but the initial costs of furnishing properties can be substantial. Additionally, there is ongoing maintenance to consider.
- **Variable rental income:** Unlike long-term leases that provide a fixed monthly income, mid-term rentals may cause fluctuations in your income because you might be at the mercy of seasonal demand or economic factors.
- **Management intensity:** While mid-term rentals are less management-intensive than short-term rentals, mid-terms still require attention. Coordinating check-ins and check-outs and addressing any tenant concerns can be time-consuming and is the reason that many long-term rental property management companies will not take on a mid-term rental. This will force you to hire a short-term rental property management team. They charge, on average, 15 to 20 percent of gross while the long-term property managers charge 8 to 10 percent, so you have to factor in the higher expense.
- **Potential for property wear and tear:** With shorter leases, there is more tenant turnover, potentially leading to increased wear and tear on the property. Regular maintenance and inspections are crucial. You must also factor in wear and tear of furniture since your midterm rentals will be fully furnished properties.

Balancing the advantages with these drawbacks is key to investing success. It might also be beneficial to consult with a local real estate expert or property manager before you dive into the mid-term rental strategy—get their opinion on the market and whether a midterm rental will perform well.

Strategy 4: Short-Term Rentals

A short-term rental is when someone leases a property for a brief time, typically less than thirty days. Since the pandemic in 2020, short-term rentals have grown in popularity on sites like Airbnb and VRBO. If done correctly, this strategy can be the most lucrative of them all. Let's say you own a property that you can charge $2,000 per month as a long-term rental, $3,000 per month as a mid-term rental, and $150 per night as a short-term rental. You would generate a total of $4,500 a month as a short-term, which is $2,500 more than a long-term rental.

In the markets where the average home price is $400,000 or more, long-term rents have not caught up to the home prices. For instance, on a $500,000 home in my hometown in Arizona, the most you could charge for a long-term rental is $2,500. Because of this, these are the markets that have seen the largest growth in short-term rentals (think Los Angeles, Scottsdale, Nashville, Austin). My wife, Camille, and I have successfully had a short-term rental property in Tempe, Arizona that we have owned since 2021 and have had a lot of success with.

Unfortunately, the disadvantage of using your property as a short-term rental is the fact that the volatility of the market can be the highest. You may have two months where your short-term rental is booked out every day, renters coming and going, and then you have two weeks with no bookings at all. Because of this, you must run numbers and evaluate the property specifically as a short-term rental before you invest. For example, here is our SOP for buying short-term rentals:

1. **Identify an area that we believe will work great as a short-term rental:** We chose Tempe, Arizona because the prices of homes were much cheaper than nearby Scottsdale, but Tempe was still central to Arizona State University, Scottsdale, and the Major League Baseball spring training facilities. (They always generate a lot of tourists.)

2. **Work with our deal finder:** Once we decided on our parameters—we wanted either turnkey properties or ones that needed a light rehab under $430,000 in Tempe—we had our deal finder send us listings.

3. **Run the numbers on AirDNA:** We had purchased AirDNA software, which pulls data from Airbnb. It shows the average nightly rental rate for a similar property and the average occupancy rate. We found that the average nightly rate in Tempe was $250, and the average occupancy rate in the area was 70 percent (meaning properties in the area were rented out for 70 percent of the year).

So we started crunching numbers. If our property is rented out every day of the year at $250 per night, we could expect to earn $91,250. However, the stickler was that 70 percent average occupancy. I recalculated what we would make if it only rented out for 50 percent of the time instead: $45,625.

Using this total, I subtracted the mortgage. Then I estimated that the utilities, cable, internet, and lawn and pool care expenses would total about $2,500 a month or $30,000 for the year. After all our expenses were paid, we would make about $15,000 a year on this property. Digging deeper, our initial investment of buying, furnishing, and doing a light rehab on the property totaled $120,000. After running the numbers, using only a 50 percent occupancy rate on the year, we would net a 12.5 percent CoC (cash-on-cash) return ($15,000 ÷ $120,000 = .125 × 100 = 12.5% CoC).

Ultimately, we felt that even if our numbers were off, and the occupancy came in lower than 50 percent, or the average nightly rate dropped, there was still enough positive profit on this deal that we would net a good return. And, if AirDNA was right and we did have 70 percent occupancy, we would make even more money! We decided to buy the property, and it ended up being a great decision for us.

One more thing—although hiring a property management company would have made this a passive deal, my wife decided to manage this particular property on her own. The good news is that by doing so, she saved us at least 15 to 20 percent of that $15,000 that would have gone to pay the property management company.

PROS OF SHORT-TERM RENTALS

- **Higher income potential:** Short-term rentals generally command higher nightly rates than long-term leases, potentially leading to increased overall rental income.
- **Flexibility for property use:** You can use the property for personal stays during periods when it's not booked, providing more flexibility compared to long-term leases. Many people do that with properties they own in vacation destinations.
- **Market sensitivity:** You can quickly adapt to market changes by adjusting the rental rates and responding to demand fluctuations more effectively than you can with long-term rentals.
- **Opportunity for seasonal peaks:** Depending on the location, short-term rentals may experience peaks during tourist seasons, events, or holidays, maximizing income during these high-demand periods.
- **Tax deductions:** Some expenses related to short-term rentals, such as property management fees, cleaning costs, and maintenance, may be tax-deductible.

CONS OF SHORT-TERM RENTALS

- **Vacancy and seasonal lulls:** Short-term rentals may face higher vacancy rates during off-seasons or slower travel periods, impacting overall income.

- **Expensive property management:** As a passive investor, you will need to hire a short-term rental property manager, and the standard fee for short-term rental management is 15 to 20 percent of gross rents.
- **Potential for property damage:** Frequent guest turnover increases the risk of property wear and tear and potential damage.
- **Regulatory challenges:** Many locations have specific regulations governing how many short-term rentals are allowed in the area and other requirements, and navigating these legalities can be complex. Changes in these regulations may also impact the success of your short-term rental.
- **Higher operating costs:** Short-term rentals often involve higher operating costs, such as utilities, cleaning fees, and furnishings, which can impact your overall profitability.
- **Dependency on platforms:** Relying on platforms like Airbnb means adhering to their policies and dealing with potential changes that could affect your business.

Strategy 5: Buy Rehab Rent Refinance Repeat (BRRRR)

First, a quick breakdown of what a BRRRR is—you *buy* a distressed property that needs a mid- or high-level *rehab*. You do the work as quickly as possible and get it *rented* as a long-term rental with (hopefully) a great tenant. You then *refinance* your loan. Because you bought the distressed property at a discount and forced more equity by renovating it, you are now able to get all or most of your capital out, and the property will still cash flow. Then you take that capital, buy a new property, and *repeat*. This is a great way to either buy deals with little or none of your own money, or recycle the same money over and over again to buy deals.

Let's do a real-life case study of what the BRRRR strategy could look like:

An out-of-state investor was presented by their deal finder an old run-down house in a really good working-class Ohio neighborhood. The house needed a ton of work, so it was definitely a full-rehab project. The investor was able to close on the house for $70,000, and comps in the neighborhood showed the after-repair value (ARV) for newly renovated properties was $200,000. What happens next?

The investor sent his contractor to the property to give a full estimate on the amount the rehab will cost and how long it will take. The contractor said he could get the job done in four months, and it would take $60,000–$70,000.

The investor reaches out to his private money lender and obtains a loan at 12 percent for 75 percent of the purchase, and 100 percent rehab cost for a total of about $140,000. This means that the investor purchased the property with $17,500 of their own money.

Talking with their property manager, the investor determines that it will take, at most, two months to get the property rented out. With all of this, the BRRRR will take about six months.

To purchase and rehab the property, the investor paid $17,500 of their own money as a down payment, but during that six-month period they also had to pay their private money lender $1,200 a month (total of $7,200). In total, the investor put in about $25,000 in total for this deal.

Now in the sixth month, the property manager signs a tenant for $1,800 a month.

With the buy, rehab, and rent portions of BRRRR completed, it was time for the investor to refinance. He did this at 75 percent of the ARV. The ARV was $200,000, so the new loan amount was $150,000 (75% of $200,000).

Let's run through the numbers:

- The private money loan was for a total of $122,500 including the 75 percent of the purchase price ($52,500) and 100 percent of the rehab ($70,000).
- All in, the investor paid $7,200 in interest payments to the private money lender and the initial $25,000 to acquire the property.
- At refinance, the investor was able to get a loan for 75 percent of the ARV, so he received $150,000. This $150,000 paid back the $122,500 loan from the private money lender and the $7,200 in interest payments. After those were paid back, the investor still had $20,000 left of the $150,000, which is almost his full $25,000 initial investment.
- The investor received all but $5,000 of his investment back at this point.

Now that the investor has refinanced and received most of their money back, he can now repeat the process on the next deal.

In the meantime, this property will generate $150 in cash flow every month after all expenses are paid. With $5,000 left in the deal, he will be netting a whopping 36 percent CoC return.

I must note that this is a fictitious deal, but I have seen several investors execute on the BRRRR strategy in a very similar manner.

> **NOTE:** When you refinance and get money back, that money is not taxable. If you were to sell the property instead, you would be required to pay capital gains taxes.

When I first started out investing in single-family properties, the BRRRR strategy was not on my radar because I did not want to deal with distressed properties, so I stuck with investing in turnkey properties.

Today, I am most interested in investing in distressed properties that need a mid-level rehab. Why? Because if it's distressed, I know I can most likely buy it at a discount and execute the BRRRR strategy. My two most recent properties in Tampa are excellent BRRRR candidates. In fact, I already completed BRR, but as of the writing of this book, I have not refinanced or repeated on these properties yet, mostly because they are cash-flowing so well.

I know at any point in time I can pull out a large portion of my capital in these deals in a refinance and repeat and buy another. My story is a great example of how the strategy you choose first does not have to be what you stick with forever. What you invest in and how you use these strategies will depend on your goals, capital, the market, and expectations at that point in time.

> **NOTE:** As of 2024 with interest rates being as high as they are, the BRRRR strategy is not working for investors as well as it used to, so do not be surprised if it's harder to execute on this strategy today.

Strategy 6: Fix-and-Flip

I have never completed a fix-and-flip, but I do know passive investors who have utilized this strategy, so I had to include it. For me, I have always been cut from the cloth that I want to hold onto my properties and benefit from long-term ownership. I feel like fixing-and-flipping properties as a passive investor is more of a gamble. You have zero control and just hope everything goes as planned.

For this reason, you must have alternative exit plans other than selling the property. Why? What if your listing agent is wrong and the property doesn't sell for as much as you thought it might? Will the plan be to turn it into a long-term rental or refinance? You may need a new agent on your team, and you need to save the deal from failing.

I believe that fixing-and-flipping is a perfect strategy for active investors because they are in the trenches of the project every day finding ways to save money.

As a passive investor, it's more of a challenge to save money throughout the rehab process when you are depending on your contractor and their team to do all the work.

For that reason, if I take on a fix-and-flip, I will partner with a contractor instead of just hiring one. I recommend this strategy for any passive investor. It's a subtle but important difference. If you partner with a contractor, they are now incentivized to keep expenses on the project as low as possible and renovate it as fast as possible. That's because, in the end, you both bring home more money if the contractor can do so.

PROS OF FIX-AND-FLIPS

- **Profit potential:** Successful fix-and-flips can yield significant profits, providing a substantial return on investment within a relatively short timeframe—typically one year or less.
- **Diversification:** Engaging in fix-and-flips allows you to diversify your real estate investment portfolio beyond long-term rentals, potentially increasing overall returns.
- **Partnering allows passivity:** By partnering with a contractor, you can maintain a more hands-off approach, relying on their expertise to manage the renovation process.
- **Shorter investment horizon:** Fix-and-flips usually have a shorter investment horizon compared to long-term rentals, providing the opportunity for quicker and larger returns.

I have found that many passive investors use earnings for fix-and-flips as capital, which increases their spread further and allows them to invest more in other strategies.

CONS OF FIX-AND-FLIPS

- **Market sensitivity:** Flipping success is heavily dependent on the local real estate market, and economic conditions can impact the property's resale value.
- **Project risks:** Renovation projects can encounter unforeseen issues, delays, or budget overruns, affecting the overall profitability of the flip.
- **Capital intensity:** Fixing-and-flipping often requires a significant upfront investment, and tying up capital in a property for

renovation may limit other investment opportunities. The alternative is to leverage construction or hard/private loans, which all are inherently riskier and have higher interest rates.

- **Market timing challenges:** Timing the market correctly is crucial for fix-and-flips. Entering the market at the wrong time could lead to challenges in selling the property at a profit.
- **Limited passive element:** Despite partnering with a contractor, fixing-and-flipping still involves more active management compared to truly passive real estate investment strategies like long-term rentals. I think this strategy can leave you susceptible to having to get more heavily involved and is another reason I typically stay away.
- **Market competition:** In competitive markets, finding suitable properties for fix-and-flip projects at a reasonable price can be challenging.

I know we have discussed a lot in this chapter, but I want to remind you that you do not have to become an expert at everything we covered. You just need to decide what exactly your niche strategy will be and build a team and SOPs based on that strategy. Decide what your niche within single-family investing will be. Then learn everything you can about it, build your team and SOPs, and you will be ready to go.

NOTE: Remember, once you buy your first property, no matter what it is, keep in mind that it's time to build on your SOPs, so refer back to that chapter when you need to.

However, if single-family investing doesn't seem to be the vehicle you want to use, you may be looking for something a bit more luxurious.

CHAPTER 10
THE RANGE ROVER
Real Estate Syndications

"Know what you own and why you own it."

—Peter Lynch, investment expert

My journey with real estate syndications started because I wanted to diversify my portfolio. I wanted to find an asset class that would give me more growth potential than the $100,000 single-family properties I was buying at the time. They were passive and cash flowed great, but they were not ideal for appreciation, and I knew that going in. However, if I could find investments that would hit my Passive Trifecta (passive, cash flow great, and appreciate well), it would help me reach the doubled TMI goal I had set for myself much quicker while building my net worth. I began exploring other vehicles that would help me get to my destination faster.

In 2016, my third year in the NFL, I began taking meetings with real estate investors who I felt were miles ahead of me. They were already investing in and buying single-family properties by the hundreds and/or multiple different types of commercial properties. In talking with these high-caliber investors, I picked up on a consistent theme: They either invested in syndications as a limited partner or purchased syndications as a general partner. Either way, every single investor I met who had a large portfolio of real estate had a portion of it in syndications. This intrigued me, so I researched what a syndication was, and the more I learned, the more interested I became.

A real estate syndication is a strategy where multiple investors pool their financial resources and expertise together to invest in larger real estate projects. These projects are challenging for an individual investor to undertake by themselves. They are common when investing in commercial properties, such as apartment complexes, industrial buildings, hotels, or development projects.

If investing in syndications was as promising as it appeared, there were sure to be other NFL players doing it too, right? I went into the locker room to talk to my teammates, but to my surprise, I could not find even one peer who had syndications in their financial portfolio at that time. As a matter of fact, many of them didn't know what real estate syndication was either.

This scared me! Syndications seemed like an incredible investment opportunity for professional athletes because we have more money than time, but why didn't any of my teammates know about it? This led me to believe that there must be something wrong with syndications that I just wasn't aware of yet, and initially, it kept me away from investing in them.

Thankfully, my curiosity never waned, and I kept reading, learning, and asking other investors outside of the football world about them. After about six months, I gained confidence in my assessment that syndications were, in fact, a lucrative opportunity that would also allow me to remain passive. I decided to trust not only my gut but also the work I put in learning about it and made my first investment.

My first syndication investment was in a multifamily property in Florida. In my typical conservative fashion, I put the absolute smallest amount of money the general partners (GPs) would allow me to put in the deal: $50,000. My goal was to test my theory and shoot my shot. I knew this investment wasn't going to change my life for the better if the investment did go as planned and I made money, but I also knew it wouldn't necessarily change my life for the worse either (if it went wrong). I didn't want to lose that money, but I was in a place where I felt comfortable taking a well-informed bet. I made that first investment and never looked back. Since then, syndication investing has remained a large part of my investment portfolio.

The Breakdown

In real estate syndications, there are typically lead investors, who are often called the general partners (the GPs). The GPs manage the project and make investment decisions. The GPs are either one company or a collection of individuals who are responsible for sourcing the deal, handling due diligence, securing financing, raising money, and managing the progress of the investment.

If it is one company taking the full GP role, that company often has different employees who take on various roles throughout the project. For instance, the person raising money from investors is rarely the same person managing the project day to day.

On the other hand, if it's a collection of investors coming together as GPs, it's typically for strategic reasons. I know a guy who is a part of the GP group on several deals, but the only role he ever plays is raising money. He has access to many high-net-worth individuals who trust his business acumen, so he leverages that to partner with other GPs who have deal operation and management strength. Then they come together as GPs to make deals work. Passive investors in syndications, known as limited partners (the LPs), contribute capital to the syndication and, in return, receive a share of the profits generated by that real estate venture. Your role as the LP in every deal is simple: bring capital and take a share of the profits.

This structure allows LPs to benefit from the potential returns of larger, more profitable real estate deals. LPs are also able to take advantage of the GPs' expertise while limiting their risk. For instance, when you buy a commercial property by yourself, the loan is in your name. When you buy a commercial property as a part of a syndication, the GPs are the ones who are taking the risk because the loan is in their name. So as an LP, your only risk is the amount of money you invested, and you can hopefully mitigate this risk by investing with good GPs who are finding quality properties and have fair deal terms.

As a passive investor, you will most likely be investing in syndications as an LP, which means you'll be contributing capital, but before you can do so, there is a major hurdle you must jump. You must become an accredited investor.

According to the U.S. Securities and Exchange Commission, an accredited investor is defined as "an individual or entity that meets specific financial criteria, allowing them to participate in certain investment opportunities that are typically considered riskier or more complex. In the United States, the criteria for an accredited investor are defined by the Securities and Exchange Commission (SEC)."[8]

---

8 "Accredited Investor," U.S. Securities and Exchange Commission, April 25, 2024, https://www.sec.gov/education/capitalraising/building-blocks/accredited-investor.

For a single person, the criteria to become accredited is having an income of $200,000 or more in each of the past two years. If married, you jointly need to have an income of $300,000 for the past two years. Additionally, there is the expectation that you will maintain that same level of income or more in the current year.

Alternatively, an individual can also be considered accredited if they have a net worth of $1 million or more, either individually or jointly with a spouse, excluding the value of their primary residence. It's important to note that entities such as certain types of trusts, partnerships, and corporations, can also qualify as accredited investors based on specific criteria.

Right off the bat, if you do not have an individual income that exceeds $200,000, an income of $300,000 with your spouse, or a net worth exceeding $1,000,000, then you can't invest in syndications—at least not right now. But becoming an accredited investor so you *can* have access to these deals is a great financial goal to put in place for yourself!

Being an accredited investor grants you access to certain private investment opportunities, such as private equity, hedge funds, and certain private placements like syndications, which are often not available to nonaccredited investors. These investments are not available to nonaccredited investors because this rule is the U.S. government's effort to protect uneducated investors from investing in deals they do not understand. While I understand the government's reasoning behind this guideline, it works as a double-edged sword because it is also preventing many Americans from having the opportunity to invest in some of the best investment opportunities our country has to offer. I do not know about you, but I do not like being told what I can or can't invest in, so even if it wasn't from the NFL, I think becoming an accredited investor would have been a priority of mine.

Why Invest in Syndications

Syndications present investors with a sophisticated strategy that allows you to diversify in asset type (office building, hotel, apartment, etc.) and location (there are good syndication opportunities across the country). Instead of allocating your capital to one deal, syndications let you spread your money into multiple different deals. This spreads out your risk and gives you a chance to optimize your return because you have a stake in several quality investments.

One of my favorite attributes of investing in syndications is what's called the preferred return, the agreed-upon amount all LPs will be paid before anybody else (including the GPs). Often, it's paid quarterly, but some GPs pay it at the end of the deal. Either way, it's earmarked as the very first capital given to investors.

After reviewing hundreds of deals, I have found that the standard preferred return is 8 percent. Barring any unforeseen issues with the investment, I know that I will receive an 8 percent return on my capital, and this, of course, is not factoring in the upside growth of the deal. I use this preferred return from all my syndications as cash flow to reach my TMI number.

For example, let's say I have $1,000,000 in syndication deals that are all paying me a preferred return of 8 percent annually, paid out quarterly. That means I will have $80,000 of cash flow from that $1,000,000 every year. This cash flow is paid out quarterly, so every quarter I should receive $20,000. When you take $80,000 a year and divide it by twelve, you see that this provides an extra $6,666 of cash flow every month. This cash flow contributes to helping me reach my TMI goals.

In my experience, the preferred return is very similar to my cash-on-cash return in single-family properties. With single-family properties, you collect your cash flow every month. At the end of the year, you calculate how much cash flow you make by adding up your monthly cash flows. You take that number and divide it by how much money you have invested in the deal in total and that will give you your CoC return.

Syndications are no different. Instead of monthly, I typically receive preferred return payments quarterly and add that amount up at the end of the year. Then I divide that by how much money I invested in the syndication. What I like about this is that the preferred return is set, whereas in single-family properties, my return may fluctuate. One year it could be 8 percent, the next 6 percent, and so on. Syndications provide a more consistent return I can count on.

Big Three

If you meet the accredited investor criteria, here are three main things you need before investing in syndications:

1. The GPs
2. The Deal
3. The Documents and Terms

Doing your due diligence on the Big Three will be essential to your success as an LP. The good news about this is that once you do it and decide to move forward with a deal, your work is done. All that is left for you to do is receive updates from the GPs on the progress of the deal and ensure that you are getting your expected distribution payments. These are payments that are agreed upon throughout the life of the project.

THE GPs

The first factor I look at when considering a new syndication is the GPs who will be running the deal. You can find a syndication that plans to buy a great piece of real estate with very favorable terms, but if the people managing the deal are not quality, the deal could still go sideways.

On the other hand, if you have some of the best GPs who are buying a mediocre project and the terms are average at best, it could still wind up being an extremely successful investment. That's because the GPs are seasoned and know how to structure great debt terms and manage a property well by decreasing expenses and increasing revenue.

No matter the property, one thing you should always expect is for unforeseen issues to arise. When you operate under the notion that something will happen, you put in perspective how important it is to select quality GPs who have high integrity and the ability to manage tough situations. There is a quote from Warren Buffett that many investors say: "Only when the tide goes out do you discover who's been swimming naked." Due to lower interest rates between 2015 and 2022, many GPs had success in buying and managing large commercial properties. As soon as the interest rates started climbing in 2023, many of these GPs fell off their high horse. They realized that interest rates were not only rising but most likely staying high for the foreseeable future. The interest rates made the tide go out, and seasoned and smart GPs were positioned well, while the others struggled and were in jeopardy of missing debt payments and ultimately losing their properties along with their investors' capital.

This is why choosing quality GPs is so important. You don't want to be tied to the guys who are naked when the tide goes out.

Here is what I evaluate about the GPs before any deal I consider investing in any deal:

- **Track record:** A GPs proven track record demonstrates competence and reliability. I assess their past performance and experience in managing similar syndications. To do this, I have them show me information on all their past syndications, and I ask them to connect me with an LP who has invested in one of them. My goal here is to see what the LP thought of the job that the GP did. I also want to make sure that those past projects are similar to the ones I am interested in. For example, if their past projects are multifamily, but they are approaching me to invest in an office building project, I am out. I want to see a proven track record in the same type of investment they are asking me to invest in.

You may find a syndication that plans to buy a great piece of real estate with very favorable terms, but if the people managing the deal are not quality, the deal could still fall apart. On the other hand, the best GPs who are buying a mediocre project with average terms can still create an extremely successful investment. That is because the GPs are good enough to turn water into wine and make a decent deal great.

- **Communication style:** Transparent and regular communication between the GPs and the LPs is vital for trust and understanding of the progress of the investment. Evaluate their communication process with investors. Ask them how often they send out updates and what their policies are on updating LPs when there has been a problem or setback. If you have access to an LP who has invested with the GPs in the past, ask them how often they received updates as well.

- **Investment strategy:** Understand the GPs approach to investments: Are they looking for A-plus locations or assets in middle-class communities? What kind of returns are they pursuing? Also inquire about their risk management: Are they throwing Hail Marys or are they okay with getting first downs? How are they securing financing, and are they locking in a fixed rate or taking their chances with a variable interest rate? Finally, investigate their exit strategies: Is their plan to sell, or will they consider refinancing and keeping the property?

Make sure you understand and agree with their overall strategy, and that it aligns with your own financial goals. If you want to double your money in the next five years or less, you probably do not want to invest with the GPs who are okay with just getting first downs. But the same goes for if you want a good solid preferred return with low risk—you probably shouldn't go with the GPs who are throwing Hail Marys.

Now that I am retired from the NFL, my main goal in the short term is to get all my different passive income streams to reach my doubled TMI number. With that in mind, when it comes to syndications, I want to get a consistent preferred return and get into low-risk deals. Once, a large ground-up development project came across my desk. It had a chance to grow my money by five times within the next five to seven years. This deal was not going to cash flow at all for any of the investors until the property was built and sold.

While I thought the project had a good chance of success and the GPs running the deal seemed legit, it did not fit my financial goals. If that same deal comes across my desk five years from now when I have reached my doubled TMI goal already, then I will be reviewing it with a completely different mindset, and maybe I will consider it.

I was once approached by a GP whose syndication plan was to rehab a 300-unit apartment complex that needed extensive upgrades and convert them into luxury units. I felt like they were swinging for the fences because the rents they were expecting to receive were above market rates for the area. They believed they could reset the market with this premium product. While they could have been right, it was another risk I was not willing to take.

To understand their approach to investments, look at the GP's past deals and returns they have done, and gauge their projections before previous deals in comparison to the results they had. A big thing I like to see is whether the GPs have multiple exit plans (ways you can make the deal work, just in case things do not go as they initially anticipated.

For instance, what if interest rates shot up like they did in 2023, and they could not sell the property for as much as they anticipated? What would the plan be? Is refinancing into a new loan and waiting until interest rates go down an option? Is there enough profit to be made on the deal that they could sell it for a lower price and still reach projections? You want to make sure they have multiple ways to succeed. If they are only counting on one specific thing to happen to make the deal work, in my mind that probability is too close to zero. I need to see multiple avenues for us to succeed on the deal, and I advise you to take that same approach.

- **Due diligence practices:** If I am about to invest in a syndication that is buying a 100-unit apartment complex, I would like to see proof that the GPs have done extensive research on the market, property, location, and so much more. A thorough analysis of potential investments indicates a commitment to making great decisions. Ask them for this information. They should have it available immediately. If they are scrambling to show you their due diligence, it's a red flag.

- **Legal and regulatory compliance:** Confirm that the GPs operate within the legal and regulatory framework. I do this by searching the name of the syndication online as well as each GP in the deal. I want to know if they have had any regulatory or compliance issues in the past. Typically, if they do, you can find information quickly by a simple Google search. The less that comes up, the better. If I see lawsuits and negative content, it's typically a sign to stay away.

I can't reiterate enough how important it is to utilize the internet and social media to investigate every GP involved with a deal. I have a friend who got into syndication with a guy who was tied to several lawsuits with LPs in the past. If my friend had simply typed in the GP's name, the lawsuits would have come up. But my friend didn't and had to learn the hard way.

Once you commit to a syndication, it's as if you are in a relationship with the GPs until the deal goes full cycle and your capital is returned. So find out beforehand as much as you can about who they are, what they do, and how they do it. As a result, you can save yourself headaches and weed out a lot of bad apples. I am a firm believer that if you can't do business with someone for a lifetime, you should not do business with them for a day. If there is something that does not add up or you do not like about one or all of the GPs, trust your gut and move on to the next one.

 **SIDELINES** _ _ _ _ _ _ _ _ _ _ _ _

Lesson Learned

Not too long ago, I made a bad decision when it comes to GPs, and it happened seven years into my journey when I was already having a lot of success. I felt as if I knew what I was doing and got too comfortable. I had spoken at a conference and was on a panel with a GP who invested in multifamily properties. Our philosophies were not the same at all. He was very much a go-big-or-go-home type of person and I, of course, am not. But I respected the fact that he had a track record of success over the past ten years or so swinging for the fences.

Despite our core differences in investment strategy, I took a chance and invested in one of his deals. Fast forward to today, and it appears that he swung for the fences and missed. He reached out to investors asking for capital because he did not raise as much money as he should have and underestimated how high and how long interest rates would go up. This GP had a variable interest rate on his construction loan, and that is ultimately what made the deal go sour. My investment amount is in jeopardy, and I just hope he can navigate the other LPs and me out of this situation and get our capital back.

This could have been avoided if I had stuck to my own rules of properly evaluating the GP before I invest and making sure we were aligned. At the time I wrote this, it could turn out to be a very expensive lesson for me. I hope you learn from it and do not put yourself in the same position.

━━ ━━ ━━ ━━ ━━ ━━ ━━ ━━ ━━ ━━ ━━ ━━ ━━ ━━ ━━ ━━ ━━ ━━ ━━

The Documents and Terms

As an LP, there are three main documents you need to learn about: the private placement memorandum, operating agreement (or limited partnership agreement), and subscription agreement. These documents provide insight into the investment structure, business plan, terms, and associated risks of the syndication. You need to use them as your main reference to review the deal, the GP, and the terms to decide whether the investment works for you.

- **Private placement memorandum (PPM):** This comprehensive document outlines the investment, including the business plan, property details, and risk factors. The GPs will typically make a detailed list of what they consider to be the biggest risks or challenges in the deal; the list may include issues like market volatility, interest rate volatility, CapEx, and so on. This document also spells out the terms of the offering, which often includes the minimum investment allowed, projected holding period, preferred return amount, how GPs and LPs will split gross profits, and so on.

  As a passive investor, you will see the PPM as the holy grail, and it will give you all the insight you need to determine whether a deal fits your needs. When I started reviewing PPMs, I was so confused! It took a number of reps and leaning on the expertise of other investors to get a good idea of what I should look for in a deal. The good news is that instead of making you go through that, I am giving you all the nuggets I have learned when it comes to evaluating a syndication and whether or not it is a good deal.

- **Operating agreement (or limited partnership agreement):** This document details the roles, responsibilities, and rights of the investors and the sponsor. The operating agreement functions as the rulebook for decision-making. It outlines major choices that require input or approval, often by the GPs. These choices can range from property management decisions to selling an asset. This agreement provides the playbook for what is and isn't allowed, so when challenges come up, the operating agreement will be reviewed. Identifying the individual in charge of resolving any issue and how that issue is resolved should also be included here.

- **Subscription agreement:** This document is the entry ticket into any syndication. It's a legal contract between the LPs and the GPs. The agreement will clarify how much will be invested, all payment details, and the confirmation by the LPs that they are accredited investors. This is the last document an LP will see, and it seals the deal, officially making them an investor in that deal.

One major issue many LPs have with investing in syndications is they have absolutely no idea whether a deal and its terms are good. After all, the PPM and other marketing materials are positioned to make it appear that it's the best deal in the world. And the GP's job is to sell the opportunity to LPs like us. It is our responsibility to analyze and decipher the deals and terms.

When I started reviewing PPMs, I was so confused! It took a lot of reps and leaning on the expertise of other investors to get a good idea of what I should look for in a deal. The good news is that instead of making you go through that, I am giving you all the nuggets I have learned so you can evaluate a syndication and decide if it's a good deal.

The Deal

Once you have evaluated the GPs and they have passed the test, it is time to evaluate the actual deal. Here are the points you should review:

> **NOTE:** When investing in syndications, you do not need to find any of this information on your own. All of it should be provided to you in the private placement memorandum from the GPs. This is one of the best features of investing in syndications. The work is done for you, and you just need to be able to analyze it.

1. **Location**: Assess the property's location, including factors like job growth, and the local economy and real estate market. Based on this information, determine whether you like the location and whether it fits with what you want in your investment portfolio.

2. **Property type**: Understand the type of property (residential, commercial, etc.) and whether it aligns with your investment goals and risk tolerance. For example, if you want to invest in multifamily properties, and this syndication is buying hotels, it is probably not the right fit for you.

3. **Financial performance**: Review the property's historical financial data and projections. Evaluate the income, expenses, and potential for appreciation. If the GPs are doing their job with the PPM, they should be painting a pretty clear picture for you as far as what the property has wrong with it financially and how they plan to remedy those issues and make it more profitable upon purchasing it. Does the picture make sense?

4. **Market analysis**: With the information you have been given, examine the market conditions, demand for similar properties, and potential for rental income and property appreciation in the future. This analysis will provide insight into the property's potential.

For example, if you are investing in multifamily syndication and other properties in the area are similar, then it is valuable to know how they are performing. Has another GP group been in the area and renovated another property similar to what your GPs plan to do? Has that property been successful or failed? Either way, knowing and understanding why is valuable information. Any property that is within a few miles and has similar qualities (such as unit count if it's a multifamily property) should be included in the GPs comparable market analysis (CMA) should be a part of their due diligence process.

To know how successful your investment property could be, you must have information on the competing properties. The good thing is this information is not for you to dig up. The GPs are responsible for not only gathering this information but providing it to you. If you come across a PPM that does not include a CMA, and you ask the GP to provide it and they do not have one, then that is a clear sign that they have not done thorough due diligence. If they have failed to do proper due diligence, *run*!

For example, let's assume another GP group bought and renovated a 100-unit property three years ago. Through your GP's

CMA report, you see that the rental rate the other GP group is charging is aligned with the projections of your GP group. To me that is a good sign—they are using direct comps to predict what they will be able to charge in rent. However, in this case, I would want my GPs to explain how the units they plan to provide will be different than the other property. What will make tenants stay at our property instead of the other one? Is there enough demand in the area for another similar property, or will ours stand out and be different in some way, drawing potential tenants to our property instead?

What if you find out the neighboring property has been owned by the same mom-and-pop owners for the past twenty years and they have not renovated the property at all? In this case, that could turn out to be a good or a bad thing. It could be a good thing because if your closest competition is a run-down mom-and-pop apartment complex, then there may be an opportunity to provide better quality housing in an area that would demand it.

On the other hand, I would want to be sure there is a demand for a renovated property in that area. I would question why another GP group hasn't bought that other property from the mom-and-pop owners yet. I would not want to invest in an apartment complex that will have no demand from tenants. In either case, the bottom line is getting a detailed market analysis from your GP; that analysis is pivotal to understanding why the syndication is, or isn't, worth investing in.

5. **Business plan**: This item acts as the strategic guide and lays out the plan for the investment. It covers the detailed strategy for executing the GP's plan. I have always viewed the PPM and business plan as working hand in hand. The PPM covers the legalities more, while the business plan dives deeper into the operational side. Things you can expect to see in the business plan are a specific breakdown of the use of all capital raised, an overview of who is on the GP team and the role they will play, and a renovation plan overview. Here is an example of what will be answered in the business plan: How long will it take for the units to be renovated? Once the renovations are complete, do they plan to refinance or sell? What is the renovation schedule? How many units will they be renovating at a time? What company are they hiring to handle renovations, or will it be in-house? Will the property be cash flow positive at all during renovations?

6. **Debt structure**: Understand the financing terms and debt structure associated with the property. Evaluate the impact of the loan terms on the overall investment. Is it a fixed or variable-rate loan? What is the length of the loan, and is there an option for an extension if the GPs need longer? For example, let's assume the GPs have a variable loan in place for two years while they renovate the property, but they face challenges and realize they need another year to finish the renovations. Will that be an option, or how will they solve this?

Here is another example of how important debt is to the success of a deal. If a multifamily syndication deal needs renovations on all the units, that means there will be more vacancies during the renovation period. Understanding this, I like to know how the GPs plan to cover the mortgage payments on the property when vacancies are higher. Will they have reserves that cover the payments, and if so, for how long? If they plan to pay from cash flow from the other tenants, then how many units can they afford to have vacant during renovation and still be able to cover the mortgage with rent payments? It's important that you know and understand the answer to questions like these because more often than not when syndication deals fail, it has something to do with the debt structure. Debt can cause a real estate deal to fall apart.

- **Variable debt:** This means the interest rate on a loan can change. If the GPs have a monthly loan payment of $100,000, and all of a sudden the rate changes and now they have to pay $150,000, that increase can bleed into the emergency reserves. The syndication can start running out of money.
- **Inaccurate costs:** The GPs inaccurately accounted for how long the deal would take to complete or how much renovations would cost. Now they need to pay the debt for a longer time. Or they may have to pay more for the rehab and can run out of funds faster.
- **Inaccurate sale prices:** The GPs predicted that they would be able to refinance or sell a property at a certain price upon completion of the rehab. Then they find out their projections were wrong, and they would not be able to sell for enough profit.

Now that you understand the important role debt plays, I would like to share the two factors I always look at before investing in any syndication deal:

1. **Interest rate:** What will the interest rate be? Is it a fixed rate or variable?

2. **Cash flow:** There are two main ways that GPs cover the cost of debt during the rehab process: through the actual cash flow of the property, or the money they raised from the LPs. It's typical for LP capital to be used as debt payment, but in that case, I always like to know how much they have put aside to cover debt payments and whether there adequate reserves. If the project takes longer or costs more than expected, did the GPs raise enough money from LPs or is there a chance they could run out? As an LP, you must know and understand their cash flow plan.

Red Flags

Not everything goes smoothly in a real estate deal. Over the years I have analyzed hundreds of syndication deals and built out my parameters of red flags to look for. Here are my ten:

1. **A syndicated split with less than a 70 percent to LPs.** This means that when the deal is complete, LPs will receive 70 percent of the profits. The GPs should receive the other 30 percent. I do not do any deals where the split is lower than 70 percent because I have found that to be the industry standard.

2. **A preferred return lower than 7 percent.** In just about every syndication I have invested in, the preferred return has been at least 7 percent. If it's lower than that, I immediately think the deal does not cash flow well, or the GP is keeping more of the money.

3. **A higher than 3 percent acquisition fee.** Some GPs are tacking on very high acquisition fees up to 4 to 5 percent, and I have found this is aggressive. It's putting the GPs in a position to make money no matter what, even if the investment goes bad. That is bad alignment, and I recommend staying away from any deal where the acquisition fee is exceeding 3 percent. In fact, in almost every syndication I have invested in, the acquisition fee was 1 to 2 percent. I only did one deal where the fee was 3 percent, and I doubt I will do another one.

4. **No clear outline of all fees.** Acquisition fees are not the only fees you will have to pay when getting into syndication, so it's important to make sure the PPM clarifies exactly what and how much all the fees are. If you ask for this clarification, and they do not have it readily available, that is a major red flag!

5. **A vague business plan.** The business plan should have thorough details and data to support the GPs' assumptions and

underwriting within their PPM. I always review the PPM and think about what could go right or wrong with the GPs' plan; I make sure I ask for their solution before I commit.

6. **The investment from the GP is less than the acquisition fee.** If the acquisition fee (3 percent max) is higher than the amount the GPs have invested in the deal, then they are making more money on the acquisition fee than they themselves put into the deal. When this is the case, I do not think the GPs are properly aligned with LPs, and I won't invest. I typically see that GPs invest at least 5 percent of the amount of money needed. Anything less than that, and I am asking questions.

7. **Rent and price assumptions.** Anytime I see assumptions where rents will go up 10 percent or more without a reasonable explanation, it's a major red flag and a high chance that they are overestimating rent growth. The same goes for annual rent growth of over 2 percent. It is risky to assume rents will grow higher than 2 percent annually.

8. **GPs receive a return before LPs get their principal back.** The LPs should receive their principal investment back before any GPs receive a return, and if that's not the case, that is a huge red flag.

9. **GPs have little experience investing in and managing that asset class.** The GPs should not only have experience investing in that asset class but also have management experience in that asset class. For instance, if it's a multifamily property and the GPs have no property management experience, it's a red flag that the property may not be managed well.

10. **An IRR (internal rate of return) higher than 25 percent.** It is *possible* but very uncommon for a syndication to have a projected IRR higher than 25 percent. I typically see IRRs between 10 to 20 percent on a deal-by-deal basis. When I see a deal that's 25 percent or higher, I assume the GPs are not being realistic, and I ask them why they are projecting such high returns. Are they predicting the property to sell for a much higher amount than what the data supports? Maybe they are right, but I do not want to see projected IRRs based on what they *hope* will happen. I want to see returns based on what we can conservatively *expect* to happen.

Is the Juice Worth the Squeeze?

I know this information can be a lot, but I promise you with time, investing in syndications can be one of the most passive ways to obtain a healthy return.

I invested in multifamily syndication with a trusted GP group that I have done several deals with. They came across a unique opportunity to buy a property in Chicago with the plan of renovating thirty of the fifty units (they decided they only wanted to renovate thirty instead of the full fifty because they wanted to get in and out of the property fast and leave some upside for the next person who would buy the deal). The previous owner was a mom-and-pop owner who neglected the property for years. The GPs felt a simple cosmetic upgrade of the interior and exterior of the property and establishing quality property management to oversee the product could more than double the revenue the previous owner was receiving.

Upon my review, I understood and agreed with their plan and loved that they were able to lock in a fixed interest rate on a three-year term for construction. They finished renovating the thirty units in eighteen months and spent a year-and-a-half stabilizing the asset with quality tenants. They sold the property and here is what the numbers looked like for me:

I invested $150,000 in this deal. There was an annual preferred return of 8 percent, so I received a total of $12,000 for three years straight for a total of $36,000 just in preferred return. After the sale of the property, I received my $150,000 back and an additional $60,000 of profit. In total, I received $36,000 in preferred return and $60,000 in growth ($36,000 + $60,000 = $96,000) in three years. My total ROI (return on investment) on this deal was 64 percent ($96,000 gain ÷ $150,000 investment). My annualized return on the investment was 21 percent. While not impossible, this high return when buying and holding single-family properties is not as easy to achieve. Meanwhile, I have invested in many syndications where I received this kind of return or better. When you consider how passive investing in syndications can be and couple it with the kind of returns from above, you will quickly see why syndications are an attractive vehicle for passive investors to choose.

Syndications are such a powerful vehicle for accredited investors, but you must truly understand how to evaluate them. As you start to get your reps looking at deals, you will continue to learn and expand your knowledge.

Syndication investing is the ultimate side hustle because of all the vehicles, it takes the least amount of time. All you need to do is find syndication opportunities and underwrite the deal and the GPs. Once you do that, literally all the work is done for you by the GPs and you just need to stay informed by reading the monthly, quarterly, or annual reports. I have mentioned multiple times that early on, I worked only five hours a week on my real estate portfolio. Not even a full hour of that time was spent on syndications—that's how easy it is.

CHAPTER 11
THE AUDI Q7
Private Lending

"When lending people money, be sure their character exceeds their collateral."

—H. Jackson Brown, Jr., author

*G*rowing up, I was a frugal kid. If you talk to my family or friends, they will say I was outright stingy. I never wanted to loan money or anything else for that matter to anyone. What was mine was mine and what was yours was yours. The irony is that now, as a major part of my passive investing portfolio, I started my own private lending company where I lend money to real estate investors.

What I realize now, which I was unable to articulate as a kid, was the fact that I wasn't being stingy for the sake of being a jerk. I had an innate ability to recognize that if I loaned something that I cherished to someone or if I loaned them money, there was no guarantee I was going to get it back (their word was never good enough for me). And I was not willing to take that risk with anything I truly valued, which, at that time of my life was money, clothes, and shoes.

The reason I am comfortable lending money now is that I learned about documents that protect me as a lender including the deed of trust (which has an asset that is pledged for the security of the loan). There is also the personal guaranty document that ensures the borrower will repay and, if they don't, I as the lender can go after their assets. I can now loan someone money, and I'm not expected to take their word they will pay me back "with interest," as they always say. With the security to take over the property or go after personal assets if the borrower doesn't pay, my perspective on private lending completely changed, and I became open to it.

What is private lending? Private lending is when individuals or LLCs provide loans to real estate investors or developers outside of traditional financial institutions like banks. Private lenders can typically offer more flexible loan terms and a quicker decision-making process than conventional lenders.

All the things you have learned in this book so far have prepared you to be great at private lending. Think about it: Increasing your spread has put you in a really good position to have money to lend. Learning the language has helped you calculate important metrics, so when you see a deal from a potential borrower, you not only know what they are talking about in their underwriting, but you can double-check their assumptions yourself. Your team members are in place, and you know what to look for on the borrower's team. Those SOPs (standard operating procedures) are created so that when you are considering lending to a new borrower, you learn what their SOPs are and can see if they have any gaps that will affect the success of your loan to them. Lastly, you learned about single and smaller multifamily investing from the perspective of an investor, you have a good grasp of what to look for, and you can determine whether a deal that a borrower presents to you is one you would consider doing. As you embark on becoming a private lender, all this knowledge gives you a distinct advantage in the space.

So how do you lend your money? You can become a private money lender (PML) or a hard money lender (HML). Before we discuss the differences, it is important to note that they both serve one main purpose: to provide alternative financing options outside of traditional banking institutions.

 SIDELINES

In Tony Robbins's book *The Holy Grail of Investing,* one of the key investment strategies he talks about is private credit, which is just another way of saying private lending. After interviewing some of the most successful investors and entrepreneurs this world has ever seen (guys like Ray Dalio,

John Bogle, Paul Tudor Jones), Robbins found that many of them have a portion of their capital in private credit. The reason is simple—cash flow reigns supreme!

You can have the best investment strategies in the world that will multiply by a hundred times in the next two decades, but you still need cash flow coming in so you can hedge your bets against downturns and have enough capital to sustain your lifestyle.

In the book, Robbins talks about lending to businesses, but the principles of lending to a business are the same as lending in real estate. The only difference is the collateral. In both business and real estate loans, the personal guaranty comes from the owners of the business or property. If you are lending money to a business, the collateral that the business puts up if they default on the loan is a stake in the company and everything that the company owns (like equipment). In real estate, the collateral is the actual property.

So, if you are hesitant about lending your money or the income it can provide for you, understand that some of the world's most profound investors today have lending as a part of their investment portfolio.

The process of obtaining a traditional loan is an extensive one. You provide a lot of financial information to the lender, including your personal and business financial statements, and personal and business tax returns dating back at least two years. You also must allow the lender to pull a hard credit report. The traditional lender then reviews this paperwork and, in addition, evaluates the property you want to buy. Then, there is an inspection report and appraisal of the property. This whole process can take several weeks, and there is minimal flexibility within it.

Additionally, many traditional lenders will not lend money on properties that they deem inhabitable—for instance, if the property is too distressed because the roof has a tree that fell on it or there was fire damage. All traditional lenders have a maximum LTV (loan to value) that they are allowed to lend up to (for many it's 75 percent), especially on investment properties. So why use a traditional lender?

Because of an extensive vetting process, traditional lenders are mitigating their risk and offer the lowest interest rates on the market. Traditional loans on single-family properties are also thirty-year-fixed mortgages that allow for amortized payments (payments are spread out evenly over thirty years and each payment pays off a portion of the principal and interest). It's hard to beat the cheapest rates and the longest terms, which is why investors are willing to jump through the lender's extra hoops. However, the problem is that many investors have situations where getting approved for traditional lending can be a challenge. For example, the borrower's credit score is low, they may need to close quickly on the property, the property is in really bad condition, or the borrower is an investor who is trying to scale, and the lender has capped the number of loans they will approve for them.

As a result, if an investor needs money but has run into dead ends with traditional lenders, they start to look for private money lenders (PMLs) or hard money lenders (HMLs). They are both great options because neither requires even half the amount of time or number of documents that a traditional lender wants. However, most private and hard money lenders are charging double-digit interest-only payments for what's called first-position senior loans. These are loans where the lender is the one who holds the primary claim to the collateral of the property, as well as two or three points (extra fees) at the beginning of the loan.

With second-position junior loans, the lender holds the secondary claim to the collateral, and a PML/HML charges somewhere between 14 and 16 percent and two or three points at the beginning of the loan. This loan is riskier because they are not in the primary position; if the borrower defaults on the loan, the second position lender has to wait until the first position has been paid out. As long as there is money left to pay out, the lender receives payment. If there isn't, the second-position lender may never get a return of capital. As a PML/HML, you want to know right away whether the borrower is looking for a first- or second-position loan and have your position from the title company before closing.

> **NOTE**: As of this writing, interest rates vary and are 100 percent dependent on the PML/HML.

Private and hard money loans are not right for every investor, property, or situation. For instance, if an investor is looking to lock in long-term debt on a turnkey property, private or hard money is not a good solution because the price of the debt is way too high. For example, if you can get approved for a 6.5 percent interest rate on a traditional loan for a long-term buy-and-hold property, taking out a loan with a PML/HML charging 12 percent does not make sense. For this reason, PML/HML are best suited for investors who need short-term funding, such as those who plan to either fix-and-flip or BRRRR a property.

The Differences

Let's break down the three key differences between private and hard money loans:

1. Source of Funds
2. Relationship Dynamics
3. Flexibility and Terms

Source of Funds

As a lender, where funds come from directly impacts the loans and terms that the PML or HML can offer to borrowers.

- **Private Money Lenders:** PMLs lend their own money, other people's money, or money from private entities to investors. I lend my own capital and will soon allow other people within my network to lend through my company as well.
- **Hard Money Lenders:** HMLs lend money from large companies, funds, banks, or institutions to investors. Over time, some PMLs grow their business to the point where they pivot and begin to bring in money from larger capital sources.

Relationship Dynamics

This is important because it affects the service you can offer to potential borrowers and how you will attract these borrowers.

- **Private Money Lenders:** PMLs typically lend in the state where they live and/or have ties. For this reason, there is a more personal relationship throughout the process. I like to meet any potential borrower for lunch before we do a loan. I also request to see the property in person before closing and throughout the renovation project. Many borrowers appreciate the personal touch of working with a PML.
- **Hard Money Lenders:** These transactions are more business-oriented and have less of a personal touch. The main concern of an HML is the collateral and the terms of the loan. Some borrowers prefer this straightforward, no-nonsense approach.

Flexibility and Terms

Ultimately, borrowers work with PMLs/HMLs because they have a unique situation with a property that they need to solve.

- **Private Money Lenders:** The PML has complete flexibility and can agree to loan terms based on their comfort with the borrower and the deal itself without needing approval from anyone else. Being able to make these kinds of decisions quickly makes PMLs an attractive option for borrowers. One of my Seattle borrowers came to me needing a second-position loan so he could finish renovations on a property. I typically do not fund any second-position loans (because they are typically riskier), but I have a great relationship with this borrower and have worked with him for years, so I reviewed the deal and agreed to fund his request within two days.

- **Hard Money Lender:** As an HML, a big portion of the funds come from larger institutional investors, so the flexibility is more rigid. HMLs tend to have standardized and set terms when it comes to the kind of loans they will fund. When an opportunity comes that does not fit within their typical loan box, they are likely to pass. Some borrowers are okay with this as long as they know exactly what the HML will/won't lend upfront.

If you want to get into private lending, it's important to understand these differences so you can decide the best way to lend your funds. You have two options: lend through a PML/HML or lend as your own PML.

Lend Through a PML or HML

You can also lend your money through another individual or company that lends money. For example, with my company, you reach out to me and my team and join our investor newsletter. You receive updates on upcoming loans that we have approved and plan on funding. You have the option to invest in these individual loans. You can fully fund the loan or only a portion of it. Whichever you choose, we agree on the interest rate you will earn on the loan and what portion my company keeps for finding and servicing the loan (managing the loan until your capital is returned). Once this is agreed upon, you sign the documents, provide the funding, and begin receiving monthly payments based on our agreement.

Every PML/HML process with investors is specific to their business and structure, so it can vary. But you can expect to go through some variation of this process whenever lending through a PML/HML. Let's discuss the pros and cons of lending through a private or hard money lender.

Pros

- **It is extremely passive.** Lending this way is much more effortless than any of the other options. All you need to do is find a PML/HML company that you are comfortable with to lend through and request access to their investor list. When opportunities come in, you review them and begin the process of funding all or a portion of the loan.

- **It is easy to diversify.** Private lending is easy to diversify because you can lend portions of your capital to several deals with the same PML/HML, or you can choose to lend through multiple PML/HMLs.

Cons

- **You will earn lower returns.** Unfortunately, this level of passivity affects what you earn. If you lend through a private or hard money lender, they will take a portion of the interest which lowers your return. For instance, I charge 12 percent and two points (that is, 2 percent) the fees that lenders charge to fund the loan) to my borrowers, but I pay my investors 10 percent. By lending through a PML/HML, you could be missing out on 4 percent or more of your profit. The thing is that many private and hard money lenders are paying their investors 8 percent. By lending through someone like this, you could be leaving up to 6 percent of the profit of the loan on the table.

  Let's see what this looks like in real time on a $100,000 loan for 12 months at 12 percent and 2 points. Jimmy decides to fund the entire loan.

  - **PML/HML 1:** Jimmy goes to a PML, and they agree to pay him 10 percent. On a $100,000 loan, he will make $10,000 in a year. He is paid monthly, so his monthly check will be $10,000 ÷ 12 = $833. Meanwhile, on that loan, the PML makes 2 percent (12% − 10% = 2%) and the loan makes two points at closing (the two points are the same as 2 percent). In total, the PML will make another 4 percent or $4,000 ($100,000 × 4% = $4,000). From my experience, this is a fair and reasonable agreement between the PML and the investor.

  - **PML/HML 2:** This PML offers to pay Jimmy an 8 percent interest rate. He will make $8,000 in a year on that $100,000 loan ($100,000 × 8% = $8,000). Jimmy's monthly payment will be

$666 ($8,000 ÷ 12 = $666). PML 2 will also make 4 percent on the interest as well as two points at closing. This adds up to $6,000 ($100,000 × 6% = $6,000).

I hope you see from these examples that if you choose to lend money through a PML/HML company, then taking the time to find one that will offer you 10 percent or higher on the interest rate increases how much you can make.

Lend on Your Own as a PML

In my opinion, lending as a PML is more suitable for a passive investor's mindset. You need to raise money from institutional investors and adhere to their lending perimeters to run the business. That can easily eat up all your spare time and turn you into an active investor. Instead, I firmly believe that being a PML is the most lucrative way to lend. It's the option I chose when I started lending and ultimately why I started my own lending business.

My strategy is to find investors who have a good track record of fixing-and-flipping properties. I foster a personal relationship with them so I understand their character and motivations, and I take the time to understand their investing business model and risk profile to make sure it aligns with my way of thinking. If these things match up, then I am ready to enter into a mutually beneficial relationship where I provide the funding they need to grow their business; in return, I charge a double-digit interest rate and points and receive regular monthly cash flow that goes toward my TMI number. The regular cash flow I make from my private lending business now exceeds the monthly cash flow I generate from all my other investment vehicles, and I only see that number improving with time.

Pros

- **You can make more money.** Now assume that Jimmy funded the same loan but did it himself as a PML. He wouldn't have to pay fees to anyone, and the entire 12 percent plus two points that was charged on the loan all goes to him. If he loaned $100,000, he would make $14,000 in a year ($100,000 × 12% = $12,000 + $2,000 in points = $14,000). Jimmy will receive his two points ($2,000 upfront) and then proceed to have monthly payments from the borrower that will be $1,000 ($12,000 ÷12 = $1,000). By becoming a PML, Jimmy finds and funds deals and makes an extra $4,000 a year on every loan compared to PML/HML 1 and an extra $6,000 compared to PML/HML 2.

Now think about the difference Jimmy can make if the loan amount increases. He will earn thousands more a year in income.

- **You have full control.** By lending to borrowers directly, you have 100 percent control over who you lend to and how much you lend to them. This gives you the ability to be as risky or as conservative as you want. For instance, I know a private lender who specializes in second-position loans—remember, this is when there is another loan has priority over the collateral in front of you. He charges 16 percent and two points, so he makes 18 percent on his money. However, because you are taking more risk on second-position loans, you can typically charge a higher interest rate. I also know someone who does the opposite and will only lend 60 percent LTV and charge 10 percent interest. Lending on your own gives you the option to decide for yourself which direction you want to go.

- **You can leverage equity in your assets.** Let's say you have $200,000 of equity in your home but do not want to refinance the property because you bought it in 2020 at a low 3.5 percent interest rate. You could take out a home equity line of credit (HELOC) and access up to 75 percent of that $200,000 of equity (which would be $150,000). When you do this, you can expect to pay around 9 percent as of 2024 on your HELOC.

One of the best features of taking out a HELOC on a property is that you are only charged interest when you pull the capital out. If you do not borrow money from it, you will not be charged. A HELOC gives you access to capital that you can choose to use only when you find an investment that pays more than the interest you will be charged.

You can lend that money to someone and charge them 14 percent (12 percent and two points). You pay your bank 9 percent interest, but since you are charging your borrower 14 percent, you make a 5 percent return on the bank's money. I scaled my lending business by leveraging my real estate portfolio this way.

However, it is very important to note that this strategy of using HELOC does not work if you are lending through another PML/HML. The reason is that if your HELOC charges you 9 percent interest, for example, and PML/HML are only paying investors 8 to 10 percent interest, in the best-case scenario you will make only 1 percent on the bank's money. In my opinion, 1 percent is too close to zero, and it's just not worth it.

Cons

The upsides of lending on your own are phenomenal, but being a PML does come with a big challenge that you need to weigh. There is no way around the fact that if you are the lender, there is more work for you to do. You have to find borrowers, create loan documents, and service the loan. This work is manageable, but it is still work and will take a chunk of your time every month as a passive investor.

All in all, I do not think there is a right or wrong way to lend your money. What your financial goals are and how much money you have available to lend will dictate which path you take. But being a private lender is a fantastic way to generate consistent passive income.

How to Become a PML

Let's state the obvious: You cannot become a private lender without having capital to invest. The good thing is it does not necessarily have to be all *your* capital. You need to figure out how much capital you have access to.

Solve Your Funding

Maybe you saved $100,000 that you can use for lending, plus there is $500,000 in equity from your personal and investment properties that you can leverage and take out HELOCs on. Now consider if you can apply for a BELOC (business equity line of credit). These operate exactly like HELOCs, but the collateral is based on the equity in your business.

Let's say you apply for a BELOC, and the bank is willing to give you $200,000 with a personal guaranty that you will pay it back. Now you have the $100,000 that you saved, access to $500,000 of equity in your properties through a HELOC, and an additional $200,000 in a BELOC, for a total of $800,000. What if you have family or friends who agree to invest in your business too, and each gives you $100,000? Now you have $1 million to lend. Don't be overwhelmed by that $1 million number. You can just start with the $100,000 savings you have as well.

Open an LLC

Once you know how much funding you have access to, open an LLC to handle all your lending. It also keeps your lending business separate from your personal finances and other businesses you may have. (Revisit Chapter 2 for information on the LLC.)

Create Loan Documents

Your loan is only as strong as your loan documents, so do not skimp on this step. Hire an attorney who has experience with real estate laws in the state you are lending in. It's not cheap, but it's very important, because your documents are what make your borrower responsible to pay you back or give you control of the asset if they don't. These documents include:

1. **Promissory note**: This is a legal document that states the borrower's promise to repay a specific amount of money to you within a specified timeframe. It outlines the terms of the loan, including the interest rates and repayment schedules.

2. **Deed of trust or mortgage**: Both are security instruments used in real estate transactions. In a deed of trust, a third party (the trustee, usually a title/escrow company) holds the legal title until the borrower pays off the loan. In a mortgage, the borrower gives the lender a security interest in the property.

3. **Non-owner occupant letter**: This letter confirms that the borrower you are lending to is not actually living in the property.

4. **Indemnification agreement**: This contract commits the borrower to compensating and protecting you, the lender, from specified losses or damages. It helps manage risk of things happening to the property and you not receiving your capital back as the lender.

5. **Term sheet**: This agreement outlines the basic terms and conditions of the loan. It serves as a foundation for more detailed, legally binding documents, such as the promissory note and deed of trust or mortgage.

6. **Guaranty**: This is a promise by the borrower to answer for the debt of the lender in case of default. It provides an additional layer of assurance for lenders.

> **TIP:** Find out if the state you are lending in is a judicial foreclosure state or a nonjudicial foreclosure state. In a judicial foreclosure state, if you must foreclose on a property, you have to handle the foreclosure through the court system. This takes more time and more money. Alternatively, if your investment is in a nonjudicial foreclosure state, the foreclosure process does not include going to court, which allows the process to go much faster and costs much less.
>
> As of 2024, foreclosures are usually nonjudicial in the following states: Alabama, Alaska, Arizona, Arkansas, California, Colorado, District of Columbia (sometimes), Georgia, Hawaii (judicial also common), Idaho, Maryland, Massachusetts, Michigan, Minnesota, Mississippi, Missouri, Montana, Nebraska, Nevada, New Hampshire, New Mexico (sometimes), North Carolina, Oklahoma (unless the homeowner requests a judicial foreclosure), Oregon, Rhode Island, South Dakota (unless the homeowner requests a judicial foreclosure), Tennessee, Texas, Utah, Virginia, Washington, West Virginia, and Wyoming. Make sure you stay up to date with national and local lending and foreclosure laws wherever you are lending.

Build Relationships with Borrowers

Once you have created your loan documents, start to build relationships with potential borrowers. I started asking my team members in the markets I wanted to lend if they knew of other investors who may be looking for private funding. I have found that if you start asking, finding people who want to take your money is easy!

I also recommend that you a) start posting on your social media that you are a private lender and are looking for investors who need funding and b) visit www.BiggerPockets.com and post on the forums that you are a private lender willing to fund deals. I have had a ton of success doing both.

Start Underwriting Deals and Lending

As borrowers approach you, you need to use everything you've learned so far to determine which borrowers and properties you want to lend to that fit your risk tolerance and goals. Then it's time to execute and fund. The worst thing you can do as a private lender is waste a borrower's time or not do what you said. Make a quick and decisive yes or no. If you say yes, do it unless some new unforeseen knowledge comes up that forces you to change your mind.

I can say with complete certainty that you can do this and remain passive.[9]

Case Study:

Let's run through a deal that I funded as a private lender so you can understand this process a bit more.

One of my established borrowers who completes fix-and-flips in Arizona approached me with a deal that he wanted funding for. Here are the numbers:

- He would buy the property off-market for $350,000 when its fair market value (FMV) was $400,000.
- He created a detailed scope of work and anticipated his renovation budget to be $50,000.
- The after-repair value (ARV) of the property, based on the comparative market analysis report my wife Camille ran (she is a real estate agent), was $520,000.
- He was an active investor with extensive experience. I have worked with this investor for many years and was comfortable funding 100 percent of the purchase price plus the cost of rehab. The only catch was that the rehab budget would be paid in four separate payments of 25 percent, and I would not distribute the next payment until I saw progress pictures of the work that was already completed. I charged 12 percent on a $400,000 loan (purchase and rehab budget) as well as the two points at closing.

  I would like to note that my normal loans are typically 70 to 90 percent LTV on the purchase price. On this specific deal, I agreed to lend 100 percent of the purchase and rehab budget because of my personal relationship and history with this borrower. He is one of only a few investors I will do this with, but I am always open to building relationships like this with other borrowers. This is why being a PML is so great. I get to make personal decisions on who and how much I will lend, and the decision is fully in my hands.

- The investor and I agreed to terms of 12 percent and two points for a 12-month loan. The payments would be made monthly, so to close, he would pay me two points, which was $8,000 on this

---

9 For more information on starting and operating a private lending business, I highly recommend *Lend to Live: Earn Hassle-Free Passive Income in Real Estate with Private Money Lending* by Alexandria Breshears and Beth Pinkley Johnson, www.BiggerPockets.com/lendtolive

deal $400,000 \times 2\% = \$8,000$. After that, every month the investor would pay 1 percent ($4,000) until he paid off the loan.

- Because I knew he was a fix-and-flip investor, I did not include a prepayment penalty in our agreement. This means that while we agreed on a one-year term, he could pay the loan off early with no extra penalties. I found this to be very helpful to my investors because many want to get in and out of properties as fast as possible. Locking them into a full year is not putting them in the best position to be successful.

Now let's take this a step further and talk about the power of lending and its compound effect. Let's assume you start with your $100,000 to invest and you can get 12 percent and two points. Let's also assume you do not need any of this cash flow for the next ten years, so everything you earn you will put right back into the next loan.

- **Year 1:** You make 14 percent or $14,000 on your $100,000.
- **Year 2:** You now have $114,000 to loan out and you make another 14 percent on that, which equals a return of $15,960.
- **Year 3:** You now have $129,960 to loan and you make 14 percent on that. This gives you a return of $18,194.
- **Year 4:** You now have $148,154 to loan and you make 14 percent on that. This gives you a return of $20,741.
- **Year 5:** You now have $168,895 to loan and you make 14 percent on that. This gives you a return of $23,645.
- **Year 6:** You now have $192,540.

> **NOTE:** The income you generate from lending is taxed as ordinary income, so always put a portion of your interest income aside for taxes.

In about five years, you will almost double your money if you roll all the cash flow you generate into more loans. This is before you even factor in that many of your loans will not last a full twelve-month term. If you mix in some six-month loans where you can increase the number of points that you charge, your earnings can increase even more.

Now I want you to think about the fact that you can also make another 4 to 6 percent by lending the money the banks gave you by leveraging your HELOC or BELOC. Not to mention you can manage all of this with very minimal expense. You do not need any employees, and any expenses that do arise you can add to the closing statement with your borrower so they will not come out of pocket.

Once you start scaling your business, you can buy loan software that will help you track all your loans. These programs can run about $1,000–$2,000 a month. That may sound like a lot when you're starting out, but you can use that same software to keep track of five loans or one hundred loans. I still like to have my lawyers look over my loan documents before I fund; this cost can be charged back to the borrower in the closing documents. I see now that I can grow my private lending business with minimal overhead.

I am a firm believer that every passive investor should have a portion of their investments allocated to private lending. It matches the mindset of a passive investor quite well.

Here are my favorite things about being a private money lender:

1. In most states, you do not need a license or any certificate to lend money. You just need access to capital and the documents. Some states do require loan broker licenses, so be sure to consult with a lawyer before deciding which states to lend in.

2. You have the final say. As I said before, I like that I have full control of who I do or don't lend to. I also determine how much interest I charge them. If I want to charge 20 percent interest I could, but the problem is whether I will be able to find a borrower who will borrow from me at that rate. I have to balance setting my loan terms and perimeters with being competitive with what other private lenders are doing.

3. The cash flow is above average compared to most investments.

4. You can easily mitigate risk. For instance, my company is in Phoenix. I never want to see one of my Phoenix borrowers stop paying and force me to foreclose on them, but if that ever were to happen, I have contacts with great contractors and could easily take over a project myself. My ability to do that is a great hedge against losing!

I believe passive investors have a distinct advantage in the private lending space. If you have taken the steps to increase your spread in your profession as well as your finances, as we discussed in Chapters 3, 4, and 5, private lending can be the piece that puts lighter fluid on your income growth.

Now that I am retired from the NFL, I am using my lending company 42 Solutions to increase my income and reach my doubled TMI goal. That excess capital lets me invest more in the other vehicles (single-family, syndications, and commercial). Private lending provides the cash flow I want now, while the other vehicles will provide long-term net worth growth. Becoming a PML can do the same for you.

By now I'm sure you see that I put a premium on cash flowing investments that are passive, and private lending is second to none in that department. The fact that you can be traveling halfway across the world and make double-digit returns on your money has always been attractive to me, and I think that is the reason why this vehicle is perfect as a side hustle.

CHAPTER 12
THE ROLLS-ROYCE CULLINAN
Commercial Real Estate

"Success in real estate starts when you
believe you are worthy of it."

—Michael Ferrara, real estate professional

Owning commercial properties is the Rolls-Royce of real estate investing. Many would love to own some, but few investors have the knowledge, resources, and most importantly, the money to buy them. Commercial properties typically cost millions of dollars (depending on location, size, and income of the asset, of course).

Commercial properties are built with the intent to make money, while residential properties are made with the intent to provide housing. Commercial real estate is *every* property that is not a single-family home (one to four units). For example:

- **Office buildings:** These are exactly what they sound like, properties designed specifically for office use.
- **Retail properties:** These include shopping malls, strip malls, and individual retail stores. Think about the plaza where you shop for groceries. If there is a strip of other stores and services next to it, those are considered retail properties.
- **Industrial properties:** These include warehouses, manufacturing facilities, distribution centers, and industrial complexes. With many people opting for online shopping today, industrial buildings to store merchandise and goods have become essential.

- **Multifamily properties:** Even though they provide residential housing, any complex that has five or more units is considered a commercial property.
- **Hospitality properties:** Hotels, motels, and other lodging facilities.
- **Healthcare properties:** When you see a medical professional, you either go to a hospital, medical office, or other healthcare-related facility. These are more examples of commercial buildings.
- **Special purpose properties:** If the buildings do not fit into other categories, the property is considered a special-purpose commercial property. For example, theaters, sports and entertainment venues, restaurants, religious facilities, and educational institutions are special purpose properties.

The Costs of Commercial

Commercial properties are priced largely based on their net operating income (NOI) and cap rates. When you own a commercial property, you can force the value of the property by increasing the NOI. Here is how:

Let's say Joe is looking to buy a strip mall with six retail spaces and three of the six are vacant. Due to the vacancies, the NOI on this property is only $200,000 a month. It could be more if it was fully leased. Joe talked to his commercial broker (who is his deal finder in this case) and found out that similar properties in the area are selling at a 5.5 percent cap rate. To determine the fair market value of the property, Joe needs to take the NOI ($200,000) and divide it by the cap rate (5.5 percent). This equals $3,636,363 ($200,000 ÷ 5.5% = $3,636,363).

He puts in an offer for $3,600,000 that is accepted. In the first year, Joe's broker found three more tenants. He can increase the rents on these vacant units, which gives him an additional $300,000 NOI a year on the property ($100,000 more than the other units already rented). Joe took this building from a $200,000 NOI to a $500,000 NOI.

Now, let's assume the average cap rate in this area has stayed at 5.5 percent. To calculate the property's value, we take the $500,000 NOI and divide it by the 5.5 percent cap rate, which equals $9,090,909. By leasing out the rest of the strip mall, Joe was able to increase the NOI by $300,000, giving him an additional $5,490,909 of capital ($9,090,909 current value − $3,600,000 purchase price = $5,490,909).

The biggest difference between residential real estate and commercial real estate is how they are priced. Residential real estate is priced solely on the selling price of comparable homes in the area (CMAs provide this). You can force the price of a residential property to go only as high as comparable homes in the area have sold for. Alternatively, commercial real estate is priced on the income it can produce. Therefore, if you can find a way to increase the NOI of a commercial property, then you can increase its value.

Seeing these commercial property prices may make you turn and run away, but do not forget a) you will be using a loan to pay for most of it, and b) if you do not have that much capital you can always purchase a piece of commercial property through a syndication and share in the profits.

We have already discussed syndications, so here are two strategies that I believe make sense for a passive investor who wants to buy commercial properties directly. They are:

- Buy multifamily properties that have five or more units.
- Purchase an office, retail, industrial, hospitality, or healthcare property and rent it out to a business on an NNN lease (a commercial real estate lease where the tenant agrees to pay for the property's operating expenses in addition to the base rent).

Let's dive into both of these strategies a bit deeper to see why I think they make sense.

Multifamily Properties

When I first started in real estate, I only wanted to invest in single-family properties. It was my comfort zone. It's the investment that made the most sense to me—everyone wants to live in a home, I told myself. As I was buying more single-family homes, I started to learn that when a tenant moved out from one of my properties, it went from 100 percent occupancy to zero percent just like that. However, if I owned a duplex and one tenant moved out, the property would go from 100 percent occupancy to 50 percent. That is obviously a way better occupancy rate, but if you think even further about this, do the math on a 10-unit property. One vacancy only drops the overall occupancy by 10 percent (from 100 percent to 90 percent). When you consider the idea of less vacancy risk and factor in that you can get one loan for one hundred multifamily units instead of one hundred loans for one hundred single-family properties, you realize the upside of multifamily investing. As I started to wrap my head around the advantages of investing in multifamily properties as opposed to single-family investments, it shifted my thinking and made me more and more interested in the multifamily asset class. With time, I understood the similarities and differences between buying single-family and multifamily properties. For example, one similarity is that you still need your core four teams in order to remain passive. A key difference is that multifamily properties offer opportunities for higher cash flow because you have more than one tenant paying rent.

I started to see the light. Multifamily properties are a great investment for passive investors because buying a property with ten units is not that different from buying a single-family home with only one unit (the loan terms are different, but at the end of the day, it's still just a loan and the process is similar).

When I purchased my first multifamily property (a six-unit property in Tampa), I went through the same processes we went over in Chapters 6, 7, and 8. I learned the language, built a team, and established SOPs. I noticed how multifamily investors talked in terms of cap rates and price-per-square-foot much more than they did in single family investing. I found myself getting more comfortable in talking about and analyzing those terms after I started looking into the six-unit property.

As far as building my team. I realized that I couldn't use the same team for single-family investments as I did for multifamily. A deal finder for single-family properties is typically not an expert in the multifamily space. They may find a deal and have some knowledge on it, but it is not their expertise.

Lastly, I had to get even more organized with my SOPs. When you have only a single-family property, you can put all your documents in one folder, and you are good to go. When you have multiple tenants in your property, it's important to have SOPs in place to track tenant lease agreements, payment schedules, lease renewals, and so on. If your SOPs with your property manager are not strong, you will run into issues managing the property.

Once I was able to tweak my language of real estate, team, and SOPs toward multifamily properties, I began to see that there were far more similarities than differences. When I went to buy the six-unit property, I realized the purchase price of the property (the most expensive property I have purchased to date) and the kind of loan I was applying for were the biggest differences between single-family and multifamily investing.

Benefits

There are several benefits of investing in a multifamily property versus a single-family one. They are:

- **Mitigate vacancy risk:** One of the biggest risks in owning a single-family or multifamily property is a vacancy. If the property has a vacancy, you are not collecting your full rent. If that's the case, you may have to pay out of pocket to cover all or a portion of the mortgage and expenses. If you have to pay out of pocket, that is an extra risk for you. An advantage of multifamily properties over single-family is that they have more tenants in place. As a result, one vacancy is less problematic for the owner. For example, let's compare owning a duplex to owning a ten-unit property.

  In the duplex, one of your tenants moves out. As a result, you now have a 50 percent vacancy rate until the empty unit rents out again. The bottom line: Your monthly rental income is now cut in half until you rent out that unit. More importantly, there is a chance the current rent you collect on the property will not be enough to cover the mortgage (assuming there is a loan on the property), and you will have to pay the balance out of your pocket until you get a tenant.

  Now let's say that in the ten-unit property you bought one tenant moves out. You are now dealing with a 10 percent vacancy. As a result, your rental income remains at 90 percent until that unit is rented out again. The good news is that in a ten-unit property, even with one vacant unit, you should still be able to cover the mortgage with the monthly payments from the other nine units.

  How does this compare to owning a single-family home with one tenant? If that tenant moves out, you immediately have a 100 percent vacancy. Unless you rent it quickly, you will need to eat the cost of any of your mortgage payments and any other expenses the property incurs (maintenance and utilities) until the new tenant moves in. In comparison, it is rare to have a 100 percent vacancy with multifamily properties.

- **Easier to manage:** Another benefit of investing in multifamily properties is that they are typically easier to manage than single-family properties. For example, owning a ten-unit property is much easier than managing ten individual single-family homes that are spread out across town. As a passive investor, I know it's the property manager who is managing these units and not you, but when you own ten individual properties, there are also ten roofs, HVACs, plumbing systems, foundations, and so on to worry about. In a multifamily property, all the big-ticket items are consolidated under one roof (or maybe a couple of different roofs if it's a multifamily property with multiple separate buildings). If there are problems with the roof, it's just one roof (or maybe a couple), not ten individual ones. Of course, there are always exceptions to the rules, but in general, you would have fewer repair and maintenance expenses owning a ten-unit property compared to owning ten different single-family properties.

- **Debt benefits:** Another benefit of buying multifamily properties is when you apply for financing. But first, let me ask which sounds easier: Have a loan for one property that has ten units in it or ten loans for ten individual properties? As a passive investor, you can save time and money by buying a ten-unit multifamily property with one loan as opposed to buying ten single-family properties with ten loans. Time-wise, you are going through the loan process once, and money-wise, you are dealing with closing costs once instead of ten times.

  There is a loan option called a portfolio loan that will allow you to put multiple single-family properties in one jumbo loan together. The problem with this loan is that it's difficult to get. Most lenders will only offer it to investors who have extensive experience. This loan is also difficult to unwind; if you ever want to sell even one property you will have to a) sell them all together since they are within the same portfolio or b) ask the lender to separate the properties to sell just one within the loan, but the lender does not have to allow this.

How to Buy a Multifamily Property

So how do you buy one? The steps of underwriting, buying, and managing a multifamily deal are almost identical to buying a single-family property. You still need team members and SOPs. The only difference is that your multifamily team will need that specialty knowledge. They include:

- **Deal Finder:** The only difference with your deal finder is that they need to be a commercial agent, not a residential one. Residential agents price properties solely on comps while commercial agents understand how to price properties based on NOI and cap rates.

An all-star residential agent with single-family properties is usually not a rockstar in the commercial space.

The best example I can give you on this is a general dentist versus an orthodontist. They both work on your mouth/teeth, but a general dentist specializes in cavities and teeth cleaning, while the orthodontist focuses on your teeth and jaw irregularities and fixing them with braces.

- **Contractor:** The ability to paint rooms in multiple units at or under budget and on time is important. One of the biggest mistakes you can make as a passive investor is assuming the contractor you use to fix-and-flip a single-family property can renovate a twenty-unit building. When vetting contractors, make sure they have completed a project at or around the size of the property you are looking to buy.
- **Property Management:** Again, you want one with multifamily experience. Can they manage that many tenants at once? A single-family property manager has to deal with only one tenant on your behalf while a multifamily manager can manage dozens or hundreds of tenants at once. The proper experience is vital to your success.
- **Lender:** Luckily, many loan providers of single-family properties have loan options for purchasing multifamily properties as well. The difference has more to do with the lending options they provide. For example, the loan length and interest rate can vary vastly from lender to lender, so if you have not already established a relationship with a lender, make sure you get multiple quotes from different lenders to see which terms work best for you.

Underwriting

As with my single-family properties, I use DealCheck to underwrite multifamily properties I want to buy. (You can find more about this in Chapter 9.) Remember, you need to account for the number of units the property has and the income they generate collectively.

Financing

Financing is the most challenging part of owning commercial real estate. For starters, you will need a down payment of at least 20 percent. On a $2,000,000 loan that would be a $400,000 down payment. To those who may be intimidated by $400,000, you must remember two things: You are not expected to have that much money now, and nobody said that the $400,000 had to be yours. It could be money you raised.

Multifamily properties are purchased with commercial loans that require lenders to conduct the same due diligence on you, the investor, but the lenders are looking much further into the NOI of the property. They will extensively evaluate the property's potential income, expenses, and overall cash flow.

Also, while most traditional loans are thirty years with a fixed interest rate, it is common to see commercial loans that are five, seven, or ten years with a higher interest rate that is either fixed or variable. Commercial loans may also have a large balloon payment (you have to pay back the full amount of the loan at the end of the loan term). The combination of shorter loan terms, higher interest rates, and balloon payments at the end of the loan term make commercial loans much riskier for an investor.

For instance, let's say I was approved for a five-year loan, and it's almost time for the loan to end. I am also required to pay it back with a balloon payment, and interest rates have shot up to 8.5 percent. My options are to either refinance the loan at a much higher interest rate (I risk not being able to cover my mortgage payments) or put more money down on the refinance to lower the payment amount. If I do not have more cash to put down, I could be forced to refinance and will no longer have a cash-flowing property. That is a tough spot to be in, but many multifamily investors found themselves in this place during 2023 when this actually happened.

By the way, considering all the factors involved with buying, financing, and owning a multifamily property, I firmly believe that this is the perfect strategy for the passive investor who wants to scale faster. How? Well, if your goal is to own one hundred units, isn't it easier to buy ten ten-unit properties than it is to buy one hundred single-family units?

Breaking Down a Multifamily Deal

Let's look at a fictitious purchase of a ten-unit property so you see how you can make money.

Sam purchased the property for $1,300,000. She put 25 percent down, which totaled $325,000 (after closing costs, it was a total of $364,000). Her renovation budget was $300,000, which the lender agreed to fund 100 percent. She anticipated the renovation to take a maximum of eight months but was hoping to finish it sooner. Assuming the renovation does take eight months, Sam is expecting a total of $82,000 in holding costs, which is the money she has to spend on loan payments and other expenses involving the property while renovations are underway.

When all is said and done, Sam is expecting a total cash investment of $446,000 ($364,000 for the down payment and closing costs + $82,000 for eight months of holding costs). The projected after-repair value of the property is $1,800,000, so she has $200,000 of equity in the property after renovations ($1,300,000 purchase price + $300,000 rehab budget = $1,600,000; $1,800,000 ARV − $1,600,000 purchase price and rehab budget = $200,000 of total equity).

All the units are two-bedroom, one-bathroom, and she can charge $1,900 per unit, which is $19,000 of gross monthly rent.

After using DealCheck to do her due diligence, Sam assumes all operating expenses will be approximately 40 percent of gross rent or $7,600 a month. The NOI on this deal is $11,400 a month ($19,000 gross rents − $7,600 operating expenses = $11,400).

In eight months when the rehab is done, Sam plans to refinance the property. She is expecting the mortgage to be $7,450. So, on this deal, Sam's monthly cash flow will be $3,950 ($11,400 NOI − $7,450 mortgage payment = $3,950). Every year this property will generate $47,400 or more. ($3,950 of monthly income × 12 = $47,400).

When this deal is complete, Sam now has $200,000 of equity in a $1,800,000 fully renovated property that has a CoC return of 10.6 percent ($47,400 of annual cash flow ÷ $446,000 of total investment from Sam = .106 × 100 = 10.6 percent CoC return).

If you decide to purchase multifamily properties, I recommend that you crawl before you walk and then run. In other words, do not buy a 100-unit complex first, even if you have the money to do so. Get your feet wet with a smaller five- to ten-unit property, then later, maybe purchase a ten- to twenty-unit property. As you learn more, you can start to buy larger projects.

Triple Net (NNN) Leasing

Investing in a commercial property that you can NNN lease (called triple net) to a tenant is the most passive way to invest in commercial real estate today. That's because, with a NNN lease, the tenant is 100 percent responsible for everything involving that property. If the roof needs to be replaced, the tenant handles it. If the parking lot lines need to be repainted, the tenant handles it. If the HVAC in the building goes out, the tenant handles it. If a car runs through the business and it needs to be fixed and remodeled, the tenant handles it. You legitimately have zero responsibilities with the property outside of collecting the monthly rent from your tenant and paying the mortgage. You can place a NNN lease on any kind of commercial property.

The good news is that you do not need to hire property management. Because it's a NNN lease and the tenant will be handling everything, there is no need to have a property manager. All you need is a broker who can help place a good tenant.

How to Find a NNN Property

The best way passive investors find quality NNN lease deals is by building a relationship with a commercial real estate broker who will be your deal finder and specializes in the type of property you want to buy. For example, if you are looking to buy a strip mall, you need to find a commercial broker who specializes in the strip mall space. These brokers can identify the best opportunities in that space and have the network where those type of deals are coming to them directly. I do not advise that you take commercial real estate investing for granted by trying to find and underwrite deals on your own.

Underwriting—Why Cap Rates Matter So Much in Commercial Real Estate

Cap rate is the most important metric in commercial real estate (arguably). The cap rate explains what your return on your money will be without any debt while factoring in ordinary operating expenses. This is important when purchasing commercial real estate because the kind of loan I can get on a commercial property may be different than what you can get, meaning I may be able to get a loan at 6 percent interest when your lender is offering you 8 percent. Or maybe I am getting approved for 75 percent LTV while you are getting offered only 60 percent LTV.

Now if the interest rate and loan amount we can both get approved for are different, then we need to be able to have a universal way to evaluate a deal—that is what analyzing a property's cap rate provides for investors. The kind of debt and terms you can get on a loan play no role in what the cap rate on a property will be, which allows investors to look at a deal objectively based on its cap rate and whether or not it's a deal they want to consider further for themselves. For instance, many investors won't even look at properties with cap rates below 5 percent.

Financing

If you are buying a property that already has a tenant and they are under contract for five more years, then the lender will likely want a five-year loan that matures with a balloon payment at the end of the lease. Lenders do not want to lend on a vacant property, so they are betting that if their loan matches up with the lease in place, their funds will be protected.

This is why at least one year before the current tenant's lease is up, you should start negotiating a lease extension or a new lease with them. Ideally, you will want the new lease signed long before the loan is due, so you can refinance into a new loan based on the new terms. If your tenant is not renewing the lease, then you want to know that as early as possible so that your deal finder can look for a new tenant to replace them before the loan is due.

The Length of Leases Varies

Unlike residential real estate where the average tenant signs a one-year lease, commercial NNN lease tenants typically sign for several years. I have found that five-, ten-, and twenty-year NNN lease contracts are the most common. If your tenant is a premier brand like our internationally known coffeehouse (retail) or a global technology corporation (industrial), I have found that they are comfortable locking in longer ten- to twenty-year leases, while the franchise businesses as well as the mom-and-pop businesses typically want the shortest lease terms available.

Personally, I do not like to sign a NNN lease with a tenant for less than five years because I factor in that the loan is tied to the lease, and I do not want to be under immediate pressure to extend the current tenant or find a new one in just a couple of years.

As a passive investor, you are very dependent on your deal finder, who will most likely be a commercial broker. You will need that person to find you the best properties to buy, help you find tenants, and work on the terms of the deal.

How You Make Money with NNN Leases

What is unique about making money with NNN leases is that the income is predictable. The reason: After you find a quality tenant and agree to terms, you know exactly how much they will be paying you every month and what your expenses will be; your only expense is the loan you have on the property. When you compare this with single-family investing or syndications, you will notice that their cash flow is not as consistent as a NNN lease month over month.

For instance, if there is a leak in the bathroom of a single-family property, and I need to have a plumber come out to repair the leak and fix any damage, then my income for that month decreases.

If that same thing happened with a NNN lease property, the owner of the business will still have to pay you the same amount regardless. Another thing to note with a NNN lease is there are fixed rent increases baked into the contract, meaning upfront I can tell my tenant that I will be increasing their rent 2 percent every year. What is great about this is if my mortgage payment stays the same, but rents go up 2 percent every year, then in ten years I will grow my income 20 percent.

One thing we must go over in terms of making money with NNN lease deals is that not all deals are treated equally. Just because you can potentially make more money with a mom-and-pop store as your NNN lease tenant does not mean that's the best route to go. You need to be mindful of what you hope to accomplish and decide if you want a safe NNN lease investment or are willing to take on more risk for a higher return.

Typically, the higher the quality of the tenant, the less your return. How? Finding a high-quality national tenant typically means longer lease terms, a potential for lease extensions, and less concern about them going out of business or not paying. Having an established quality tenant takes a lot of risk off the table. Properties with these tenants are usually highly desirable, so they cost much more to buy, which negatively affects your annual return. You are paying more for a property with a quality tenant than you would for a less-established tenant.

On the flip side, let's say you find a great deal on a commercial property where the current tenant is a barber, a local tenant who may be reliable but is considered lower quality and unestablished. You can probably get a great deal on the purchase of that property because the barber is unestablished. Because of the lower quality tenant, you are rewarded with a cheaper purchase price, which equates to a higher annual return. But you must understand that you are taking more risk with that barber than you are with an established national tenant. The cap rate on the local barbershop is going to be higher than the cap rate on an international insurance corporation building.

But be careful! Do not jump at buying a commercial property because the cap rate is projected to be 10 percent when another location is 5 percent. You need to understand that higher return typically comes with more risk, and you need to consider whether that risk is worth taking or you would rather invest in more stability with the established tenant.

> **TIP:** Having a lawyer who is experienced with commercial real estate transactions is pivotal. Honestly, you can get away without actual legal representation when buying single-family properties and investing in syndications, but when it comes to commercial real estate, having a lawyer is a must. The lawyer will help review the loan documents for you, ensuring you understand all the terms and how they will affect your business. The lawyer will also draw up the tenant lease and ensure you are legally protected.

The main reasons I would invest in a NNN deal are passivity, predictability, and risk control. I love finding deals that are passive, and these fit the bill. Having one tenant pay me every month for ten years is ideal. Once the tenant agrees to terms, I know how much I will get paid every month, and I know the tenant is responsible for everything. That predictability is helpful. Finally, I get to determine how much risk I will or will not accept from the tenant. If I want safety, I can pursue an established national tenant. If I want a higher return, I can pursue a local small business.

However, the things I am most concerned about with NNN lease deals are:

- **They require large sums of money.** Quality commercial properties can cost millions of dollars, depending on the location and size of the property.
- **Vacancy.** If/when a tenant decides to move out and no longer leases my building, I am worried about the length of time it will take to find another tenant to replace them. What if the lease agreement and the loans are coming to an end, and I can't find another tenant before the balloon payment is due?

Overall, if I can find the right commercial property, the benefits outweigh the downside, making NNN leases a great option for the passive investor.

Commercial real estate as a side hustle is not something I recommend you jump into right away. It's essential that you have the right knowledge, team, and SOPs in place, otherwise you'll put yourself in a position where it takes far more of your time than anticipated or, even worse, you make mistakes and lose money. Instead, I recommend investing in the other vehicles first; when you have built your real estate portfolio, you can begin to grow into owning multifamily and/or NNN lease properties. In other words, use commercial as the next steppingstone after the other side hustles we have discussed.

SECTION IV CONCLUSION

Let's recap: First, you need to sharpen your ax by learning the language of real estate, thinking about who you will need on your team, and establishing the SOPs you should have in place. Once you have done that work, it's time to get crystal clear on the best real estate side hustles out there and make a decision on which one fits your goals and personality the most. I recommend that you start with one vehicle and really commit to it before adding a second one to your plate.

As you start to build out your portfolio, you will hit a point where you have to make a pivotal decision: How much is enough? This is what I will work on answering in the next section; it's time to scale up!

SECTION V
SCALING UP

Scaling up isn't just about increasing numbers; it's about expanding vision and unlocking new possibilities.

- **SCALE UP**
- Take Action
- Prep for Action
- Increase Your Spread

The transition from taking action to scaling up can take years, maybe even a decade or more, so I do not want you to think that after one to three years, you should be scaling up to a massive portfolio of properties and/or investments. Things typically don't work that way, but I can say with certainty that if you stay the course, you will undoubtedly hit a point where you must make a decision on how much you will scale up your real estate side hustle.

Congratulations! You're about to scale up and getting to this point is a big deal!

The impact that scaling up your real estate investing journey can have on your life is profound, and I do not just mean by the amount of dollars and cents you can make. Deciding to scale up my business while I was still playing in the NFL has also given me purpose. I retired in 2023, and I already had the benefits of more income, investments, and a higher net worth. But what I didn't expect was how much joy my business would bring me. I have always held to the idea that football was what I do and not who I am, but passive real estate investing is what feels like reality for me. Investing in real estate is the light that still shines for me, even though I am no longer under the lights on Sundays.

I heard my eldest daughter, Camryn, telling one of her friends that I used to play football, but I buy houses now. She told her friend that I stopped so I could spend more time with her and her sister. That little comment meant the world to me. She is only 5 years old as I write this, and she said that when she grows up, she wants to sell homes like mommy (Camille, my wife, is a real estate agent) or buy homes like daddy.

As you think about scaling up, understand the impact it can have on you and those you love.

You have put in the work to set yourself up for what's coming—it's time to chase your next benchmarks. The truth is that just taking action by making a few investments could get you to your first benchmark (your fixed expense number)—and maybe even your second benchmark (your TMI number)—just like it did for me. But if you desire to double your money and double your fun, this next section is going to help you do that. It will show you how to achieve your doubled TMI benchmark and achieve the pinnacle of your passive real estate journey—your abundance number. It's time to earn more income, buy more properties, and invest in more deals—let's scale up.

To me, scaling up means growing or expanding your investments passively and safely. Many investors think that scaling is just growing in size (more properties or investments) when in fact, as a passive investor, it's about growing efficiently, effectively, and most importantly, safely. You never want to invest or scale the wrong way by losing all your money with bad investments or turning your investing into a full-time job instead of a side hustle. Scaling up as a passive investor is a fine balance of growing your investments, your ownership in properties, and your cash flow without adding substantially more work or risk for yourself. Otherwise, you potentially push yourself into becoming an active investor, which you don't want.

Through my journey, I have found there are three objectives you need to meet to successfully scale up your real estate side hustle. They are:

1. Set Clear Goals and Timelines
2. Refine your Knowledge, Team, and Procedures
3. Buy Back Your Time

Put the work in on these steps, and you will be scaling up in no time!

CHAPTER 13
SET CLEAR GOALS AND TIMELINES

"People who are crazy enough to think they can change the world are the ones who usually do."

—Rob Siltanen, marketing expert

In Chapters 3, 4, and 5, you learned about passive income goals and benchmarks on your journey. They are:

1. Passive Income Covers Your Fixed Expenses
2. Passive Income Covers Your TMI
3. Passive Income Covers Your Doubled TMI
4. Passive Income Leads to Your To-the-Moon Number

If you have already begun implementing what you've learned in this book so far, you have a better idea of what is possible. Have your goals changed at all? Maybe if you make enough passive income to cover your fixed expenses and your TMI you might want to stop there. Or do you want to continue on your journey and achieve the third benchmark, where your passive income covers twice your TMI? Maybe you achieved that too. Now you're staring at that to-the-moon number, but you're okay with pulling back, satisfied with what you've already accomplished. All of that is perfectly fine. However, if you're ready to catapult your success and your income, read on.

In 2019, I was a year into my contract with the Detroit Lions, and I had significantly increased my spread and was making really good money. I used a lot of that money for investments, and by the end of the year, I had reached the TMI number that I had set for myself years earlier. The consistent cash flow from my portfolio of properties in Ohio and Kansas City, as well as the preferred returns from my syndication investments, was generating enough to sustain my lifestyle.

I thought I would be done with investing and ready to pack it in at that point. After all, I was living my NFL dream and had hit my TMI number. But something inside of me began to shift. Up to that point, I felt like I had a *good enough* mindset. I always thought that as long as I could hit my TMI number, I knew I could have a pretty good life and not be too stressed. But once I accomplished that, I couldn't help but feel like *good enough* was simply not good enough for me anymore. Ideally, I wanted a higher quality of life than what my initial TMI number was, and once I saw what was possible through passive real estate investing, I asked myself, *Why stop now?* (If you want to learn even more about me and the importance of mindset in my life, you should read my other book, *It All Adds Up.*)

With this new mindset, I shifted my TMI number to what I ideally wanted it to be in a perfect world. For example, if your current TMI number is $10,000 a month and you hit it, that's great! But wouldn't you like to have more money to spend and do things you like? If so, maybe your ideal TMI number is $15,000 a month.

Once I established what my ideal TMI number was, I saw a path of immense growth and began to think even bigger. That is when I created the doubled TMI and the abundance benchmarks. With these new benchmarks in place, the idea of scaling up was born, and I went on a journey to turn my current portfolio into something much bigger.

The next question I asked myself was, *How do I grow my portfolio bigger to reach these benchmark goals?* Which vehicle do I use to get there? For me, that answer was a combination of single-family properties, syndications, and private lending. It was 2020 when I committed to scaling up, and I proceeded to make several strategic moves.

We (my wife, oldest daughter, and I) moved out of the three-bedroom, three-bathroom condo that we had purchased and moved into our long-term home. The condo was brand-new and in a great location. We bought it for $325,000 with 25 percent down ($81,000) and had a mortgage on the property that totaled $1,425 a month. The HOA fee was $400 a month, so total monthly expenses were $1,825 ($1,425 mortgage + $400 HOA = $1,825). After checking rental comps, we were confident that we could charge $2,500 in rent at the time. Our monthly profit would be $675 ($2,500 rental rate − $1,825 total expenses = $675 of monthly cash flow). This property cash flowed $8,100 a year ($675 monthly cash flow × 12 months = $8,100 yearly cash flow). The CoC return on this property is 10 percent ($8,100 yearly cash flow ÷ $81,000 of initial down payment = .1 × 100 = 10% CoC return). Today, we charge $2,800 for rent and the value of the condo is almost $600,000. It's been an incredible investment for us.

A year later, Camille and I purchased our Airbnb property in Tempe, Arizona. Go back to Chapter 8 to see the numbers on that deal, but we have been seeing 10 percent or higher CoC returns on that property since we purchased it, and the value has increased by $80,000 since then.

In 2020, I had a total of thirteen units in my portfolio. One in Indiana (I sold this property at the end of 2020), six properties in Ohio, and six properties in Kansas City. Since then, I have purchased another twelve units—eight in Tampa, and four in Tennessee. These purchases include two full rehab projects in Tampa, which was a first for me.

In January 2020, I had twenty-three syndication investments, but as of March 2024, I have forty-two. I have almost doubled the number of investments I had since deciding to scale.

In 2020, I funded my first private lending loan for $200,000. As of March 2024, I have funded sixteen loans for a total of $3,600,000. The capital funding these loans so far is a combination of my own funds as well as HELOC and BELOC credit, and it's bringing in six figures annually.

The combination of these investments was a part of my plan to scale up and has allowed me to reach my doubled TMI number. I did not try to do this all at once but instead did one deal at a time and let things build up over time to where they are today.

Once you start to have success in real estate investing, you might decide to scale up in your own way. Maybe you are content with reaching your TMI number, or maybe it was not a good representation of how much you want to make.

For example, let's say Sarah calculated her TMI number as $10,000 a month. After opening her eyes to how much money she could make in real estate and considering what she wants her ideal life to look like, she would like to be able to spend more than $10,000 a month. Ideally, the TMI number she wants is more like $20,000 a month.

That changes everything for Sarah. If she kept her TMI goals at $10,000 a month, she'd be selling herself short because she knows that she wants more. Acknowledge what you want. It's okay to want to make more. The great thing about setting an even higher TMI number is that if you fail, you fail forward. Let's say that Sarah works hard to build her real estate portfolio, but she only manages to generate a TMI of $15,000, not the $20,000 she wants. She might have fallen short of her ideal $20,000 goal, but she still put herself $5,000 a month ahead of the original TMI goal. She's failing forward.

 **SIDELINES** _ _ _ _ _ _ _ _ _ _ _

Breaking Down How Sarah Scales Up

Sarah's initial TMI was $10,000 a month ($120,000 a year), and she has already reached that benchmark. She wants to make a TMI of $20,000 a month. She is a lawyer making $500,000 a year, and because her spread is so high she is saving an average of $380,000 a year. Sarah's work as a lawyer is very demanding, so she only wants to invest as an LP in syndications. She reached her initial TMI through preferred returns from syndications. She does the math and realizes she can reach her ideal TMI number in as little as four years if she invests the full $380,000 of extra income she makes into syndications that give an 8 percent preferred return. That's $380,000 a year × 4 years = $1,520,000 of total money invested. $1,520,000 of total money invested × an 8 percent preferred return = $121,600 of additional annual cash flow added. $121,600 of annual cash ÷ 12 months = $10,133 of monthly cash flow. When you add this $10,133 of cash flow on top of the $10,000 TMI goal she already reached, you can see that it will take her four years and a total of $1,520,000 invested to reach that ideal TMI number. I must note that this is only factoring in Sarah's 8 percent preferred return. These syndications should generate much more growth over the life of the investment, which will only improve her financial position.

In this example, you can see that Sarah's ideal TMI number is very much in reach for her.

Do you want to stay in the career/job you have now for another ten years? Twenty years? Thirty years? When I signed a three-year contract with the Arizona Cardinals in 2020, I knew that by the end of that contract, I would be nearing the end of my career. With that in mind, I needed to start scaling up so I could be in the best position possible when that day came. This timeline played a major role in not only what I invested in but how much and how fast I invested. If you are in a situation where you plan on working for another ten to fifteen years, you have a much longer runway to scale up. Playing in the NFL, I never had that luxury.

How fast do you want to reach your benchmarks? I love the quote, "Be quick, but never hurry." It's okay to have a sense of urgency when it comes to reaching your benchmark goals, but it is unrealistic to expect to reach them overnight. It's also a risky mentality. Trying to achieve something great so quickly often leads to cutting corners, which leads to mistakes. Mistakes in investing means losing money, and Warren Buffet's number-one rule for investing is "Don't lose money!"

Also, think about what your timeline is for retirement. What do you want passive real estate investing to look like for you at that point in your life? Do you want it to stay the same, or will you be willing to dedicate more time to real estate investing? That five hours a week that I put aside for real estate investing while I was in the NFL is now twenty hours since I retired because I knew that if I only worked five hours a week with no day job, I would be bored out of my mind. This extra time has allowed me to accomplish far more than I used to.

It is important to note that changing the number of hours you dedicate to real estate is completely up to you. I decided to increase mine when I retired from the NFL, but you may retire and decide you want to travel the world or golf every day. What is beautiful about this is you get to plan ahead and design what you want that life to look like. Then pick the passive investing vehicles that align with your goals most.

However, do not use your timeline as an excuse to rush the process. I grew a lot from 2020 to 2024, but by that time I felt I had set a great financial foundation for myself and had a good path forward. I heard stories of people rushing to scale and getting into risky investments or turning themselves into active investors in the process. Be ready to execute, but never rush the process.

Having an idea of what you want to happen and when is essential to designing your plan to scale up. Now it's time to chase the lifestyle you want, and if you fall short, it's still a win because you will be so far ahead of where you started!

Cash Flow or Appreciation

What matters more to you—cash flow or appreciation? I am cut from the cloth where I valued pursuing passive income/cash flow until I reached my doubled TMI goal. Once I hit that benchmark, I shifted my focus to appreciation. It's rare to find an investment that hits the Passive Trifecta:

It's passive, cash flows well, and appreciates.

For instance, if you like the option of private lending, your focus is on cash flow. There is no appreciation in lending. You lend money so a borrower can buy a property, get great cash flow, and then pay you back so you can lend money out again.

If you want to invest in single-family homes in expensive markets, appreciation matters more to you right now, and you need to be willing to live with lower cash-on-cash return.

If you happen to find an opportunity that hits the Trifecta, always take advantage of it. In most cases, you will have to choose your focus. That decision will impact the decisions you make as far as the vehicle to invest in and what strategy to use.

Do not worry, though. Instead, gain comfort in knowing that what your focus is today does not have to be what your focus is later, especially when you are planning to scale up. For instance, meet James, a 22-year-old who plans on having a career for the next twenty to thirty years, at least. He decides that his real estate focus will be on investments that appreciate over the next ten to fifteen years. In that time, James hopes the value of his investments will increase three to four times.

This mindset may lead James toward investing in commercial real estate or syndications where he pursues A-plus quality and location investments (properties of great quality and location tend to appreciate the best over time). With a ten- to fifteen-year horizon, James may be less concerned with the short-term cash flow and have his eyes set on the appreciation potential over that time.

Ten years later, James is now in his thirties, has a family, and wants to retire in the next five years or so. Over the past ten years, his investments in commercial real estate and syndications grew exponentially, just as he planned. But with early retirement on his mind, James wants to begin scaling up. He now values cash-flowing assets more and plans to use the growth in equity from the past ten years to invest in his own single-family properties that he will buy with a low LTV (loan-to-value ratio) and private lending. Between the two, he will have enough cash flow to reach his doubled TMI benchmark. He can retire early.

"Be stubborn about your goals and flexible with your methods."

—Author Unknown

When I first started investing in syndications, I thought I had found the best investment vehicle that was ever invented. All I had to do was bring the capital, and I got to share the profits. Yes! For years, I thought I would primarily invest in syndications for the rest of my investment career. But then 2020 came and I started to consider scaling up and evaluating exactly how I could/should do that. In the end, I felt that buying more single-family properties and getting into lending should play a pivotal role in scaling my investment portfolio.

While I still think syndications are a great investment tool as a side hustle, I have grown to appreciate owning properties myself and private lending on my own, which gives me control of what happens with the assets I own or loans I provide. The thought of more control of my investments has made me make sure I keep a good balance of my properties, private loans, and syndication deals. By the way, more control does not necessarily mean more time. As I mentioned before, syndications are about as passive as it gets, but that does not mean the other vehicles aren't passive and great side hustles as well. In my phase of life today, I prefer a side hustle that I have a little more control of.

Now that I am retired from the NFL and putting in twenty hours a week on real estate, scaling up for me will entail all four vehicles. Buying single-family properties will remain my bread and butter. I will select GPs that I continue to invest in with syndications. I will grow my lending business, and when the right opportunity comes, I will purchase another multifamily property or buy my first NNN deal. Once you establish your own goals and timelines, decide which vehicle(s) you will choose to scale up and get you there. Just remember to give yourself room to grow and evolve.

⭐ SIDELINES

When deciding to scale up, you must always keep in mind the current real estate market conditions and what makes sense for you. For instance, in 2023 interest rates were high, so whenever I underwrote a deal with debt, it did not pencil out as something I should consider buying. Because of that I pivoted and bought the six-unit property fully cash because I got it way below market value. That was the only property I purchased in 2023, and I will take some of my capital out when interest rates drop. Additionally, I leaned into lending because I recognized that as one of the best uses of my money while finding good deals on my own was tougher. My last pivot in 2023 was deciding not to invest in any new syndications. A lot of GPs were struggling to perform as they promised to their LPs due to the high-interest environment. Instead of putting more money into any syndications, I waited it out to see what deals played out well versus those that didn't. Because of the current real estate market, my goals didn't change, but how I accomplished them did. I had to pivot with my method, and I think that is a major role in scaling up.

Reestablishing your goals and timelines gives you a clear picture of what scaling up needs to look like for you. The worst thing you can do is begin scaling up for the sake of scaling up. Due to social media, many passive real estate investors feel the pressure to own hundreds or even thousands of units or lend a much larger amount of money, but they aren't evaluating exactly what they are hoping to accomplish.

Fight the urge to scale up for no reason. Have actual intent and, most importantly, a destination in mind. That destination, coupled with the flexibility in method, will put you in a position to succeed. Remember, what you are doing today may not be the best path for you to scale a few years from now. How you get to your goals and timeline may need to shift along the way.

Now that you know where you are headed, it's time to redefine the knowledge, team, and procedures that will help you execute your scaling-up plan.

CHAPTER 14

REFINE YOUR KNOWLEDGE, TEAM, AND PROCEDURES

*"Do the best you can until you know better,
and then when you know better, do better."*

—Maya Angelou, memoirist and poet

There is a huge difference between being book smart and street smart. In passive real estate investing, book smart is the person who has learned all the knowledge they need, put together a tentative team of all-stars, and has an idea of the procedures they will implement. The book-smart person can talk the talk, but they do not have enough experience to actually walk the walk. The street-smart person is the one who has been in the real estate investing trenches every day getting real-life experience. The street-smart person has built out a team and SOPs. While this is great, the street-smart person is learning as they go and is susceptible to making a lot of mistakes.

The most lethal passive investors I have come across are the ones who are both book smart and street smart. You don't know what you don't know. That means if you don't have the book smarts, you are in jeopardy of making mistakes due to that lack of education. On the other hand, if you lack investing experience, there are likely gaps in your ability to execute efficiently because of a deficiency in experience. When you take the time to be both book and street smart in real estate, you are in the best position to successfully scale up.

Once you learn and experience passive real estate investing and it's time to scale up, you may have to refine what you are doing in each of your vehicles (single family, syndications, private lending, and commercial). Here are a few examples of how I have refined my investments to scale up:

Single-Family Investing

When I bought properties in Ohio and Kansas City, I bought in cash and did not use a lender. As my portfolio grew, I started to use debt and added that team member. For me, that looked like securing traditional loans, but last year since I retired, I had to refine my team members again. I identified lenders who would lend to me, even though I am no longer a W-2 employee. I am technically considered unemployed since retiring from the NFL, and traditional lenders do not like working with the unemployed. Additionally, using cash to buy properties was not a sustainable solution for me to scale up, because I would eventually run out of money. Therefore, I was forced again to refine my knowledge and team and figure out how to refinance my properties and pull out capital so I could use it to fund future purchases.

In 2022 and 2023, I began to see fewer turnkey properties that reached my 8 percent CoC return requirement. This left me with two choices. I could either accept the lower return or refine my team and procedures to support renovating properties. I chose the latter and worked to build a new team in Tampa to handle renovations.

In 2024, I began investing more in Arizona because that is where I call home. The problem is the Arizona market is hot, and it's challenging to find a good deal even while working with all-star deal finders. I have been underwriting deals regularly and nothing seems to pencil well enough. My solution to this is to hire a virtual assistant, an independent contractor who can go directly to the local Phoenix auction and bid on homes that are in foreclosure on my behalf. Hiring a VA requires me to refine my SOP process and add in procedures to ensure that the VA can execute exactly how I expect them to. Luckily, you can now bid at auctions online at www.auctions.com, so I will be utilizing that site as well as my VA to try to get deals far below market value.

Syndications

After the mistake I told you about in Chapter 10, where I invested in a syndication that will likely fail, I took a step back and reevaluated my SOPs for investing in syndications. I recognized that over the years, after having so much success in syndication investing, I became too lax in my due diligence process of GPs and deals overall. Then I became worried that more of my deals would turn out to be failures. This new perspective led me to refine my SOPs when it came to choosing GPs and deals I would invest in. I have made far fewer syndication investments over the past year and a half, and I plan to stick with the GPs who have under promised and overperformed in the past for me and have an investing strategy that perfectly aligns with my risk tolerance.

Private Lending

Starting my own private lending company was my big refining moment. Up to that point, I felt as if I were just winging the private lending, but now it has become a point of emphasis for me. I read books, listened to podcasts, and took meetings with as many people as I could within the private lending space, understanding that I still had a lot to learn. Then, I hired a lawyer to work with me on all my private lending deals.

Commercial Properties

My six-unit property in Tampa is my only commercial property to date and I have owned it for just about a year now as of March of 2024. I am not yet ready to scale up in the commercial space, but I am becoming more book and street smart in the space with every passing day, which I think will position me well when I am ready to start scaling up here.

I cannot predict the lessons that you will learn as you begin to scale or what the right way is for you because it will depend on your own goals and objectives. However, the foundation of being able to scale will require that you refine your knowledge, team, and procedures. There is no way to scale effectively as a passive investor if you cannot do this.

My Biggest Mistake in Scaling Up

One of my old college coaches used to always say, "If you see a little, you see a lot. If you see a lot, you see nothing." The point he was trying to make was that as players we needed to focus on the small details and get good at the fundamentals. If we did that, everything else would fall into place. For me, as an outside linebacker, if I paid attention to the quarterback, running back, and wide receivers who were all around me, I would likely be late to respond when the ball was hiked, and I would have less chance of beating the offensive tackle and sacking the quarterback. However, if I stayed laser-focused on the ball, as soon as it moved, I would move, and I could then put all of my attention on getting past the offensive tackle, who was trying to block me, so I could get to the quarterback.

I have found that this lesson has an immense crossover to real estate investing. Let's say that James from Chapter 13 wants to invest for appreciation and decides to focus on NNN lease commercial deals. But he was constantly getting sidetracked by looking at single-family fix-and-flip properties. He is seeing too much, which equates to seeing nothing. As a result, he is putting himself in a position to fail at both of them.

The foundation is set for refining your knowledge, team, and procedures, but the biggest problem you will face is your focus. Many passive investors (including myself) learned about the four vehicles and tried to hop in the car and drive more than one at the same time. I do *not* recommend that. Unfortunately, this was a mistake I learned the hard way when I started scaling up in all four vehicles at once.

Since 2020, I have invested in over twenty new syndications, purchased twelve new units, and loaned out $3,600,000 to investors. Luckily, I had good teams and SOPs in place so none of these vehicles failed me, at least not completely. But truth be told, I was cutting corners left and right. The biggest corner I cut while scaling in all four vehicles was failing to track my income and expenses and accurately monitor how each investment was performing.

Instead of focusing on the performance of my current portfolio, I dedicated *all* of my passive investor time to scaling up, buying the next property or investment, and reaching my next benchmark goal. I was ignoring the portfolio I already had.

Even worse, I got cocky with my knowledge, team, and procedures and started just going through the motions. With my single-family properties, I stopped combing through my monthly reports from my property managers. With syndications, I stopped looking at owner statement updates from the GPs and didn't keep in touch to ask questions about the progress of each deal. With private lending, I stopped reading each loan document myself to ensure that everything was right. With commercial real estate, I got lazy and stopped building and refining my team so I could find my next deal.

As a result, none of my portfolio was performing as well as it could have because I had dropped the ball. I got so enamored with growth that I forgot to make sure that what I already had was excelling. I was seeing way too much, so essentially seeing nothing. I dialed everything back.

First, I scaled up my private lending business, which brings in a great deal of cash flow, sustains my lifestyle, and gives me additional capital to invest. About fifteen of the twenty hours that I currently work go toward my private lending business as of now (I don't expect that to always be the case). The other five hours are for scaling up my single-family side of the business. I will use the cash flow from private lending to purchase at least one to five properties a year. This balance of private lending and single-family investing is the perfect combination for this stage of my life.

The cash flow is essential because I am now retired from the NFL, but the only problem with private lending cash flow is that it will be taxed as general income. Being able to use the excess cash flow to buy single-family properties and also take advantage of the tax benefits of owning properties is a good mix for me. What I also like about this strategy is not only will private lending fund the single-family investing, but I can also leverage the equity in the single-family properties and use the HELOC funds to lend out more money.

Interestingly, I have decided that I will not be scaling up in syndications for the foreseeable future. Instead, once I scale up further in private lending and single-family investing, I will consider scaling up in commercial properties. The great thing is that if over the next few years my lending business and single-family investing portfolio grow, the capital from both will help me get into quality commercial deals. This is my path for scaling up and is subject to change in the future, so do not feel like you need to copy this exact strategy. Figure out the scaling up vehicle(s) that make the most sense for you and your goals.

If you take one thing away from the lesson I learned, it should be to skip over the phase where you try to scale the four vehicles all at once. Instead, pick one or two that work well together and for you, and make sure they are aligned with the new benchmarks you set a chapter ago.

There are Riches in the Niches

The final step in refining your knowledge, team, and procedures is identifying your niche strategy within the vehicle(s) you have chosen, so you can have a focused vision in scaling up. As I explained, my scaling up focus is single-family properties and private lending, but here is an example of my niche strategy within each:

Single-Family Investing

- I want to purchase one-to-four-unit properties in Arizona's Maricopa County. My focus is to find properties below market value that need a light or mid-level rehab. I would like to BRRRR the properties and turn them into mid- or short-term rentals.
- I will also purchase one-to-four-unit properties in central and south Florida with an emphasis on Tampa. I will look for properties to buy below market value that need a light or mid-level rehab and BRRRR them just like I will do in Arizona. The goal is to have the same type of property profiles in both markets. The only difference is that I plan to place long-term tenants in this market and not use short- or mid-term rentals.

Private Lending through 42 Solutions:

- I will lend to experienced real estate investors who are fixing-and-flipping single-family or multifamily properties in Maricopa County. I prefer properties that are $1,000,000 or less, and my standard loan length is twelve months.
- I will identify experienced investors in other markets across the country who are fixing-and-flipping single-family or smaller multifamily properties that I have a trusted personal relationship with and lend to them. I will not publicize 42 Solutions as a national private lender as I want Arizona to be the focus.

I do not have my specific niche for scaling up with syndications or commercial real estate yet, but here are two examples of how you might do it:

- **Syndications:** You could focus on investing in multifamily syndications in the Midwest with experienced GPs.
- **Commercial real estate:** Your niche could be mom-and-pop NNN lease tenants in strip malls in the state you currently live in.

The bottom line is that deciding which vehicle you will use and the niche strategy you will implement within that vehicle is essential to your success. First, it allows you to get highly concentrated on the exact knowledge, team, and procedures you need to put in place. For instance, now that I have chosen Arizona and Tampa to be focused markets for me, I can dive deep into learning as much as I can about those markets. I will get into the nitty-gritty of which cities, neighborhoods, and even streets are best to invest in. By having a niche, it also allows me to build out a very specific team. I can find the best contractors in the Phoenix market and vet them out. Once other all-stars see how active I am in their market, it will attract other team members, which will allow me to improve my team or have backup options. It will also help me develop procedures that are hyper-specific to my niche, and that will help scaling up happen efficiently.

Lastly, identifying a niche strategy within your vehicle(s) also gives you the power to say no and not waste your time with any investment opportunity that does not fit your criteria. It is easy to get bogged down with so many different opportunities that waste your time and take you away from what you should be focused on.

As you round out your scaling-up strategy, there is one last thing you must do: Buy back your time.

CHAPTER 15
BUY BACK MORE TIME

"If you really want to grow as an entrepreneur, you've got to learn to delegate."

—Richard Branson, business magnate

Remaining passive has to be your North Star if you are going to have a real estate side hustle. To do this and scale up at the same time, you need to buy back more of your time. After all, when you go from owning one unit to owning ten, twenty, or one hundred units, there will be more to manage. And, twisting the proverb made famous by Stan Lee's Spider-Man, "With more volume comes more responsibility." So now you have a decision to make when it comes to handling those additional responsibilities. Will you:

1. Scale up and cut corners?
2. Scale up and hire help?

I truly believe that the only way a passive investor can scale up without cutting corners is by devoting more time to the business. This goes against being passive, which we already established was non-negotiable. To successfully handle these responsibilities, you need to hire more people.

Okay, those options were kind of rhetorical, but for two years I scaled up by cutting corners. I talked about how I cut corners in the last chapter, which included not staying on top of my financials (income and expenses) as I should have and not tracking and reviewing my current portfolio performance.

I also wrote about not diligently documenting my paperwork. As a result, most of my passive investing time was spent being reactive. I would check my email in the morning and spend the day addressing whatever felt most pressing to me at that time. I was spending way too much of my precious passive investor hours on low-dollar task items, like responding to emails, looking for insurance documents my lender asked me for, and so on. I should have been spending time on the high-dollar task items that grow and improve my portfolio, like reviewing the numbers on my next deal, making sure my current investments are performing as expected, strengthening my relationship with team members, and improving my SOPs.

On the other hand, I struggled with the idea of hiring help because I did not want to spend the money. It seemed like a frivolous expense. Additionally, trusting a stranger to come into my life and have access to my financial information and administrative tasks was hard to wrap my head around. Once I realized that I was stifling my ability to scale up because I was wasting time being reactive and doing all these little tasks that I could have handed off to someone else, hiring someone won out. Plus, by not having help, I was taking more risks with my money. How? I was mismanaging things and handling way too much, so I was overwhelmed and making the wrong decisions as I tried to do everything myself.

So, let's take a look at how each real estate investment gets busier as you scale and then who you can hire to help you buy back some of your time.

Single-Family Scaling Up

When I invested in my first property, it was easy to handle. Every month, I received a statement from my property manager, reviewed it, asked questions on anything that seemed unclear, and made sure the amount of money I was told I would receive each month was the same amount that was in my bank account. That was it. But as I scaled to twenty properties in different markets across the United States, I now had five property managers, each sending me a monthly statement that I needed to review. That took up even more of my very limited time.

Having more properties also means dealing with more repairs and more vacancies. Even though the property managers handle the day-to-day of these, you still need to be aware of what's happening and review repair bills and new tenant information. This shouldn't take a significant amount of your time, but it still is more responsibility.

And then there's more lender paperwork that comes along with buying more properties. I purchased my first twelve properties fully cash, but when I went from twelve to twenty properties, I decided to refinance the properties I already owned (take a mortgage out on them) and use that leverage to buy new properties. Now I was dealing with multiple loans. Applying for these loans on the front end and then managing them to make sure they are paid on time as well as verifying property taxes and insurance, and so on doesn't take too much time, but certainly added even more responsibility to my already crowded plate.

Now add thirty, fifty, and even eighty more units to the mix. Can you run one hundred units exactly how you ran one? Sure. But the reality is that there will probably be more responsibilities that come along with those tasks, and it will be a challenge to keep this all as passive as you want it to be without help.

Syndications Scaling Up

Investing in syndications is interesting because they are private holdings. It's not like investing in the stock market where you check your brokerage account for the value of the investments, read reports, and get immediate updates.

With syndications, you sign the paperwork, commit yourself to the investment, and wire the funds to the GPs. Some GPs, but not all, have robust online portals that allow you to sign in and get all the investment information in one place. Keeping track of one syndication is easy as you just wait for monthly or quarterly updates.

But imagine owning a stake in forty syndications. I have invested in more than that over the last decade and, after the first year, I realized how difficult it was to keep track of everything—when you invested, when the deal is supposed to pay you, when to review the quarterly update and more. If you're not organized or have someone to organize this information for you, it can quickly get overwhelming. I've forgotten some of the names, locations, and even business strategies of what the GPs plan to do with the property of certain deals I invested in years ago.

Having to find missing information and being unorganized is a waste of my and your time when we are trying to be passive investors. Buying back some of your time helps you to stay organized and, in turn, scale faster.

Private Lending Scaling Up

Before I started my company, I had already been lending money for three years to two investors I trusted in the Arizona and Seattle markets. I had built relationships with both of them over a few years before they approached me, offering to pay me a nice return if I lent them money to scale their fix-and-flip business.

Honestly, when I started as a private lender, I did not have all the documents I laid out for you in Chapter 11. I didn't know what most those documents even were back then. Instead, I leaned on the expertise of my borrowers and, luckily, they were experienced, good, and trustworthy people who showed me the processes and coached me on how to properly lend to them. The process wasn't difficult or time-consuming, so I started lending to them on more deals. Of course, when I was just lending to the two of them, I found private lending to be extremely easy. They would send me the deal; I would make sure that I liked their plans and agree to send them the money. Then I would collect my interest checks every month.

I operated this way with them for three years. When I started my own business and publicly promoted it to businesses and investors who were looking for funding, many reached out to me in a frenzy. I had opened the floodgates and there was no way to stop it. Before I knew it, trying to underwrite every potential borrower and deal and still remain passive quickly became a huge challenge. I had to set parameters and cut back on how many new borrowers I would even consider lending to. While I wanted to scale my business, I learned that I needed to do it marginally and bring in help, otherwise I would turn my lending business into a full-time job for myself, and that was *not* passive.

Commercial Scale Up

My only commercial asset as of this writing is the six-unit property I own in Tampa, so I have not personally scaled up commercially yet. But I know enough about the business and have talked to enough investors that I can share my concerns. The main concern is that commercial investing will threaten my level of passivity because I will need to bring in more capital to scale. I am not in a position where I can buy several commercial properties on my own, so I will need to either raise money from other investors or take on partners. Regardless of what I choose, it is an additional responsibility that will take more time and effort. If I do not have the right people in place around me, that work will fall on my shoulders. All of a sudden buying multifamily or NNN lease properties becomes way more time-consuming than I intended it to be.

Who to Hire?

Life gets busy. You're already working a full-time job, raising children, going to school, looking after your aging parents, and doing a million other things, so trying to fit in more responsibilities is tough. Fortunately, as you begin to scale, others can help you keep all of this under control, which will allow you to keep real estate as a side hustle. Yes, you are using part of your income to pay them, but in the long run, you are saving time, which will then allow you to scale even more. Let's start with two people you can bring on board:

Bookkeeper

You already have, or will have, team members in place handling so much of the work for you, but you also need a bookkeeper who will keep track of where every dollar is going. Hiring a bookkeeper will eliminate almost all the administrative work you need to do regarding money: reviewing monthly statements from property managers, tracking the investments and dividend payments from syndications, tracking bank statements, managing the books and all the income and expenses in your private lending business, and tracking commercial assets too.

I did not like how much time it took me to do this on my own, so instead of doing the right thing, I just started to slack off for more than a year. I learned a big lesson from that because as time passed, I couldn't even tell you with confidence how much money I made or spent during that time, and once I realized this, it wasn't a good feeling. That was when I decided that it was time to hire a bookkeeper who could manage and oversee all my personal and business finances.

Now my bookkeeper gives me monthly profit-and-loss statements that show exactly how much money came in and went out for every single one of my properties, businesses, and even in my personal life. The money I pay my bookkeeper is worth it because it has allowed me to stay informed about my finances and has given me so much of my time back that I can now focus on other things.

I want to be clear here. Even when you hire a bookkeeper, you are still solely responsible for your personal and investment financial well-being. The bookkeeper is the experienced employee, but *you* are still the boss, and whether things are good or bad, it is ultimately your responsibility.

You will need to work with your bookkeeper to ensure all the information that is being collected is accurate and a clear and true representation of your financials. I can do this by reviewing the profit-and-loss statement that my bookkeeper produces for me every month for every one of my investments. If a property is showing less profit one month compared to the previous month, I call up my bookkeeper to look into it further and to reach out to my property manager if need be.

Bookkeeper vs. Accountant

Many passive investors make the mistake of thinking they do not need a bookkeeper because they already have an accountant, but they are mistaken. The role of an accountant is much broader than a bookkeeper. An accountant's main role is to help you with tax planning and tax filing for you personally as well as for your businesses and investments.

A bookkeeper gets into the daily financial details of your business and personal life to accurately track all your data and report back to you. My bookkeeper makes my accountant's job much easier when it comes to filing taxes because I now have detailed reports for every month and the entire year.

Executive Assistant

An executive or virtual assistant (EA or VA) takes many administrative tasks off your plate, freeing up your time. They both serve the same purpose, but let's clarify the difference between the two.

An executive assistant is someone who works directly with you and only you. They typically work in an in-person office setting. If you work from home, they may come to your home to work with you but can also work remotely. A virtual assistant is someone who may have you and several other clients they work with at the same time. A virtual assistant works only remotely and can be located anywhere in the world. It is common for businesspeople to hire foreign VAs because they are typically cheaper than finding a VA within the United States.

Here are just a few examples of what they handle:

- **Scheduling:** An EA can handle your entire schedule based on the parameters you give. Think about all the time that you spend trying to squeeze in meetings, appointments, and family time into your day-to-day schedule. Leaving it up to someone else means all you have to do is check your schedule every day and see what you have going on. Of course, you are free to adjust it as necessary, but you do not have to do all the upfront legwork.

- **Email management:** If you are anything like me, you spend far too much time trying to get your inbox to zero. What if someone handled all of that for you? Your EA can handle both your business and personal emails. All you have to do is set up SOPs so they know which emails you want to handle versus the ones that they can handle for you.
- **Travel coordination:** An EA can manage personal and business travel based on the SOPs you set. These guidelines include your favorite places to stay and airlines to fly as well as your account numbers so you can rack up points and earn free travel. For example, my EA will know that I only want to stay at Marriott Hotels so I can build my Bonvoy points and earn free rooms.
- **Underwriting support:** Your EA can help gather and package the information you need when you are underwriting a property that you want to invest in or lend on. This part of investing is a time suck, so having help buys you back valuable time.
- **Document organization:** With any aspect of your investing and scaling up, there are many documents, both physically and digitally. Your EA can create filing systems to keep track of all of them.

> **NOTE:** There are many companies where you can hire a bookkeeper or EA/VA, but I have personally used www.belaysolutions.com. They will first do a client intake meeting to pair you with a bookkeeper or assistant who is best suited for your personal and business financial needs. I found a high-quality bookkeeper through them that I hope to work with for many years to come. (They have not paid me to say this.)

The Holy Grail

As a passive investor looking to scale up, I think the holy grail is hiring a bookkeeper and assistant. It's the last piece that truly puts you in a position to have a real estate side hustle efficiently, effectively, and safely. You may be fearful of the cost and letting these pros into your personal and professional life, but from my experience, the results are worth overcoming the fear. Your portfolio will grow, and your quality of life will increase. One day you will wake up and see that your largest financial dream is now your reality, and you are living your ideal passive investor life.

CHAPTER 16
LEAVE A TRAIL

"Someone is sitting in the shade today because someone planted a tree a long time ago."

—Warren Buffett, businessman

Having a full-time job or career while also trying to build a real estate empire is hard, but that's fair. Think about it, if this was easy, everybody would be doing it. I now hope the knowledge I have reluctantly gained through every mistake and stumble along the way puts you in a position to succeed faster and better in your passive investor journey. I hope you draw on and learn from my stories and experiences and make new mistakes and face new challenges.

I am fully aware that trying to learn all the information I packed into this book in the first go-round is like trying to drink water out of a firehose. That's okay. Soak in what you can and then reread it as often as you need to. My hope is that you pick up something different every time that can help you on your path.

Your journey will be much different than mine was, and by no means do I expect you to do things exactly the way I did. This blueprint is not intended to be a hard and fast step-by-step guide. Real estate investing does not work that way. You need to take the core principles, concepts, and knowledge that you learned and apply them to your situation. After all, we are two different people. Our goals, financial situations, and risk tolerances are all different. What I hope for you is that you take this framework and blaze your own trail with it.

Flip the Bag

In my first book, *It All Adds Up*, I dive into the concept of flipping the bag in your life. It's based on a story in the book of Matthew where there are three servants and a master. The master is going on a trip and entrusts one of the servants with five bags of gold, another with two bags of gold, and the last with only one bag. He tells each of the servants to go invest the money the best they know how and when he comes back, he expects a report.

The man with five bags of gold invested it and turned the five bags into ten. The man with two bags of gold invested it and turned it into four bags. The man with one bag of gold was lazy and scared, so he did nothing with the money. When the master returned, he returned with just one bag. The master denounced the last man, and he is never spoken of again. Meanwhile, the men with ten bags and four bags were praised and lifted up.

The lesson I took from this story, and what I want to encourage for every one of you is this: Whether you are the man with five bags of gold or one, it does not matter. What matters is what you do with what you have. Play the cards you have been dealt in life to the best of your ability, and turn five bags into ten, two bags into four, or one bag into two.

I like reading autobiographies, and in 2023 I read Kevin Hart's, Phil Knight's, Rick Ross's, and Stephen A. Smith's. The one common thread I took from each of these incredibly successful individuals is that they all came from humble beginnings. One could argue that they were all similar to the man with one bag of gold. Instead of doing nothing with what they had, though, they flipped the one bag to two. The great thing is that they did not stop there. They turned two to four, four to eight, eight to sixteen, sixteen to thirty-two, thirty-two to sixty-four, and so on. When you look at each of these guys today, it's hard to fathom that the amount of success they have had in their lives and careers all started with flipping that first bag and then doing it over and over.

When I was young, my dad flipped the bag in his life and became a professional football player who played for thirteen years in the NFL. Growing up, people looked at me as the kid who had it easy because my dad played pro football and that always bothered me. As an adult, I still feel that people write off my success on the football field as well as what I have done as a passive investor because "I had it easy as a kid." I can't deny that my dad making it to the NFL didn't benefit me. I can't deny that making good money in the NFL didn't benefit my passive investor journey. But like the man with five bags of gold, I want to be judged by what I have done with what I've been given. I took my situation and all the blessings in my life and have attempted to maximize them to the best of my ability, and I want people to look and judge me based on that.

This is all that matters.

I do not know what your current life situation is, what you do for a living, how much you make, what background you have in real estate, or anything else, but what I do know is there is someone in this world who comes from a similar background as you who found a way to flip the bag in their life and are extremely successful today. Now it is *your* turn.

Doing so as a passive investor provides an incredible opportunity for you, and I am confident that you can do it. Remember the story about the two guys who needed to cut down a tree—one got to work while one took the time to sharpen his axe? If there are times when it feels like you are not progressing, keep in mind that you are still preparing to do something great by sharpening your ax.

My challenge to you is to take action. Not next year, not next month, and not even next week. Make the decision today that you will start your real estate side hustle. Pick an amount of time you can devote to real estate weekly, and make sure you get that time in every day. Whether you are increasing your spread, reading real estate books, or listening to a podcast, commit to the hours that fit with your lifestyle and stay consistent. With time, these hours will build upon themselves, and you will be amazed at where you end up. I'm excited for you!

Leave a Trail

I am a firm believer in leaving a trail for the next person, so I can't end this book without asking you to do the same. As you read this, someone is already preparing to be in your shoes one day. They may benefit from your journey as direction on how they, too, can change their life by having a real estate side hustle. The real estate industry is full of active investors growing and scaling large businesses and talking about how passive investing is not a thing. It's the responsibility of people like you and me to prove them wrong. Having your cake (investing in real estate) and eating it too (doing it passively) is possible, and I challenge you to share your journey and your story as you go.

In fact, many active investors with their large portfolios grow old and try to pass their actively run portfolios down to their kids to find out that their kids don't want anything to do with their business. I have heard and seen this happen many times already in my life and what I find is unique about passing on a passive investing portfolio to my kids is I will not be asking them to take over something they have to actively manage themselves. As passive investors, we will be passing on a portfolio but more importantly a strategy and perspective about passively investing in real estate. That strategy will allow our kids to pursue whatever ventures their hearts desire while having a portfolio that is providing them cash flow along the way.

My hope for both your family and mine is that having a real estate side hustle becomes a staple among our families and friends.

I hope that is a part of the legacy we can leave!

ADDITIONAL RESOURCES

Podcasts/YouTube

The BiggerPockets *On the Market Podcast*, www.BiggerPockets.com/podcasts/on-the-market

Real Estate Investing with Coach Carson, www.coachcarson.com/coach-carson-podcast

The Weekly Juice Podcast, www.weeklyjuicepod.com

Books

The Lifestyle Investor: The 10 Commandments of Cash Flow Investing for Passive Income and Financial Freedom by Justin Donald

Lend to Live: Earn Hassle-Free Passive Income in Real Estate with Private Money Lending by Alex Breshears and Beth Johnson

The Hands-Off Investor: An Insider's Guide to Investing in Passive Real Estate Syndications by Brian Burke

The Small and Mighty Real Estate Investor: How to Reach Financial Freedom with Fewer Rental Properties by Chad Carson

Long-Distance Real Estate Investing: How to Buy, Rehab, and Manage Out-of-State Rental Properties by David Greene

The E-Myth Revisited: Why Most Small Business Don't Work and What to Do About It by Michael Gerber

Software

BiggerPockets Pro

DealCheck

QuickBooks

Stessa (BiggerPockets Pro members get a free Stessa account)

BestPlaces

AppFolio

RentCast

Google Maps

ACKNOWLEDGMENTS

I would like to thank my wife, Camille, and daughters, Camryn and Carsyn, for being patient with me throughout this writing process. I was up late many nights and missed a few play sessions to get this done, but that would not have been possible without your support.

I would like to thank Lisa Iannucci and the entire BiggerPockets Publishing team—Savannah Wood, Katie Miller, Kaylee Walterbach, Winsome Lewis, Jamie Kilingensmith, and Greta Shull—for not taking it easy on me throughout the writing process and pulling more out of me, even when I thought there was nothing left to give.

I want to thank all my team members across the country—financial advisor, accountant, bookkeeper, assistant, content manager, deal finders, property managers, contractors, lenders, general partners, and mentors. When you read this book, I know there will be aspects of my story that you are connected to or resonate with, and I just want to thank you for helping me. I would not have any of the success in real estate without you all!

God Bless!

ABOUT THE AUTHOR

What's up guys? My name is Devon Kennard, and I am a nine-year National Football League veteran, professional real estate side hustler, and author. I was born and raised in Phoenix, Arizona, and after spending the first fifteen years of my adult life in other states, my family and I moved back to Arizona and, except for the hot summers, we love it here. During my time in the NFL, I built a real estate portfolio that, as of May 2024, consists of twenty-seven personally owned assets, forty-five real estate syndications, and $5 million in monies loaned out through my private lending company, 42 Solutions.

In 2023, I wrote my first book, *It All Adds Up: Designing Your Game Plan for Financial Success,* in which I challenged my readers to re-create their version of the American Dream, and I showed them what the impact of making consistent financial progress over time can have on their life.

Today, my biggest passion professionally is building financial success for my family and myself by passively investing in real estate and helping others do the same. I plan to share and help as many people as I can with these books and my speaking engagements, while I continue to learn and grow too.

Thank you for reading *Real Estate Side Hustle,* and I look forward to the day I get to meet you in person. Please head to www.devonkennard.com and subscribe to my weekly newsletter on real estate and investing.

REFERENCES

"Accredited Investor." U.S. Securities and Exchange Commission. Last modified April 25, 2024. https://www.sec.gov/education/capitalraising/building-blocks/accredited-investor.

"Consumer Expenditures—2022." U.S. Bureau of Labor Statistics. Last modified September 8, 2023. https://www.bls.gov/news.release/cesan.nr0.htm.

Dickler, Jessica. "62% of Americans Are Still Living Paycheck to Paycheck, Making It 'The Main Financial Lifestyle,' Report Finds." CNBC. Last modified October 31, 2023. https://www.cnbc.com/2023/10/31/62percent-of-americans-still-live-paycheck-to-paycheck-amid-inflation.html.

Hetler, Amanda. "Definition ChatGPT." TechTarget. Last modified June 2024. https://www.techtarget.com/whatis/definition/ChatGPT.

McMillin, David. "Median Home Prices in Every State." Bankrate. Accessed July 17, 2024. https://www.bankrate.com/real-estate/median-home-price/#expensive-states

SUPERCHARGE YOUR REAL ESTATE INVESTING

Get **exclusive bonus content** like checklists, contracts, interviews, and more when you buy from the BiggerPockets Bookstore.

www.BiggerPockets.com/bookstore

Real Estate Deal Maker: Winning Strategies to Find & Finance Successful Rental Properties in Any Market
by Henry Washington

The two biggest problems in real estate are finding properties and funding deals—and the solution to both starts here. Are you ready to master the art of finding remarkable properties and securing the funds to seal the deal? Look no further.

wwwBiggerPockets.com/ReadDealMaker

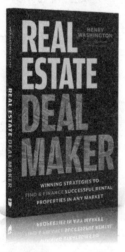

Scaling Smart: How to Design a Self-Managing Business
by Rich Fettke and Kathy Fettke

Are you ready to create passive income, free up your time, and grow your business without sacrificing your sanity? In *Scaling Smart*, RealWealth founders Rich and Kathy Fettke distill more than twenty years of business strategy into an approachable guide to scaling a successful enterprise.

www.BiggerPockets.com/ReadScalingSmart

Looking for more?
Join the BiggerPockets Community

BiggerPockets brings together education, tools, and a community of more than 2 million like-minded members—all in one place. Learn about investment strategies, analyze properties, connect with investor-friendly agents, and more.

Go to www.BiggerPockets.com to learn more!

 Listen to a **BiggerPockets Podcast**

 Watch **BiggerPockets on YouTube**

 Join the **Community Forum**

 Learn more on **the Blog**

 Read more **BiggerPockets Books**

 Learn about our **Real Estate Investing Bootcamps**

 Connect with an **Investor-Friendly Real Estate Agent**

 Go Pro! Start, scale, and manage your portfolio with your **Pro Membership**

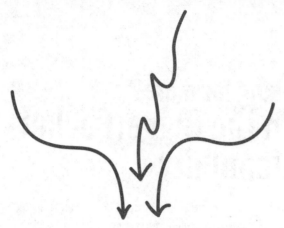

Follow us on social media!

Continue your learning and start taking action with
a FREE BiggerPockets webinar! Join Dave Meyer and follow
his steps to get your first rental property in the next 90 days.
Head to www.BiggerPockets.com/90dayweb.